Na

Blue Ridge Parkway

Nature Guide to the Blue Ridge Parkway

Ann and Rob Simpson

FALCONGUIDES

GUILFORD, CONNECTICUT
HELENA, MONTANA

AN IMPRINT OF GLOBE PEQUOT PRESS

FALCONGUIDES®

Copyright © 2013 Morris Book Publishing, LLC

ALL RIGHTS RESERVED. No part of this book may be reproduced or transmitted in any form by any means, electronic or mechanical, including photocopying and recording, or by any information storage and retrieval system, except as may be expressly permitted in writing from the publisher. Requests for permission should be addressed to Globe Pequot Press, Attn: Rights and Permissions Department, PO Box 480, Guilford, CT 06437.

FalconGuides is an imprint of Globe Pequot Press.

Falcon, FalconGuides, and Outfit Your Mind are registered trademarks of Morris Book Publishing, LLC.

All photos © Ann and Rob Simpson/www.snphotos.com.

Original mapping provided by the National Park Service, © Morris Book Publishing, LLC.

Text design: Sheryl P. Kober
Project editor: Julie Marsh
Layout: Sue Murray

Library of Congress Cataloging-in-Publication Data is available on file.

ISBN 978-0-7627-8095-2

Printed in the United States of America
10 9 8 7 6 5 4 3 2 1

Contents

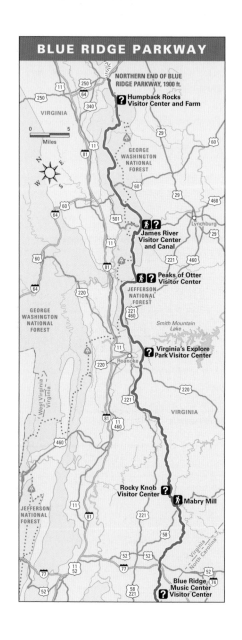

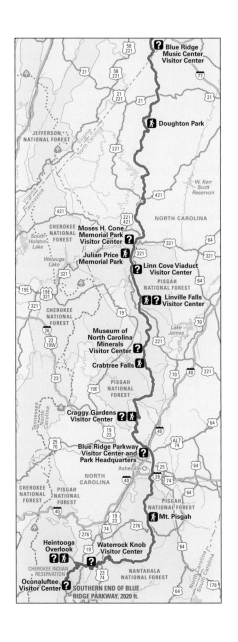

Acknowledgments

Many thanks to the superb professional personnel and volunteers of the Blue Ridge Parkway who have dedicated their lives to preserving the natural resources of the Parkway and to sharing its natural wonders with visitors. We would especially like to thank Bambi Teague for sharing her wealth of knowledge about the Parkway's natural history. Thanks also to Peter Hamel and Tina White for their helpful comments about current Parkway information. Special thanks go to Karen Searle of Eastern National for her support and encouragement for this project. Our thanks also to Dr. Susan Mills and the staff and members of the Friends of Blue Ridge Parkway for their continued support of the interpretive and educational mission of the Parkway. Our sincere appreciation goes to the naturalists and staff at Grandfather Mountain and Mount Mitchell State Park for their dedication in helping to preserve these unique habitats. We would also like to thank all the staff at FalconGuides and Globe Pequot Press, especially Jessica Haberman and Julie Marsh, whose support and efforts made this National Park Nature Guide series a reality.

We would like to dedicate this book to our family, who has supported us with encouragement and understanding during the research, writing, and photography of this nature guide.

To the reader, we hope that this guide helps to open your eyes to the wonders of nature and in doing so will generate a spark of love for the plants and animals that rely on us for their continued existence in important natural habitats such as the Blue Ridge Parkway.

The Parkway provides protected habitat for wildlife such as the colorful indigo bunting.

Shared Responsibility

The protection of the Parkway and surrounding region is an immense task, with much at stake. Decades of eroding budgets have reduced staffing and made it more and more difficult to maintain the Parkway's aging and considerable infrastructure to monitor and preserve its many natural and cultural resources, and provide educational services for visitors. The trend is undeniably clear: Fewer staff members must confront mounting threats and try to carry out a dual mission of preserving the Parkway and serving the visiting public. They cannot do it alone. Their success will depend on mobilizing an army of concerned citizens. **The Parkway of tomorrow will be defined by the extent to which people today are willing to speak out on behalf of the Parkway and to invest in its future.** Fortunately, many nonprofit partner groups now work hand-in-hand with the Parkway staff. While these organizations have differing missions, they share an overarching goal: to preserve and enhance the national treasure that is the Blue Ridge Parkway.

Blue Ridge Parkway Association: Promotes travel along the Parkway and provides print and electronic information to visitors about adjacent accommodations, attractions and communities. blueridgeparkway.org

Blue Ridge Parkway Foundation: Raises funds to support many Parkway programs and projects. brpfoundation.org

Friends of the Blue Ridge Parkway: Promotes volunteerism and leads tree plantings to screen adjacent development. blueridgefriends.org

Blue Ridge National Heritage Area: Helps operate the Parkway's Visitor Center (Milepost 384) and promotes the preservation and enjoyment of western North Carolina's cultural and natural heritage. blueridgeheritage.com

Eastern National: All you need to do is shop at nonprofit stores in Parkway visitor centers to enjoy your visit more, support visitor center staffing, and generate cash donations to the Parkway! easternnational.org

Carolina Mountain Club: Provides trail maintenance at the Parkway's southern terminus. carolinamountainclub.org

Conservation Trust for North Carolina (ctnc.org) and the *Western Virginia Land Trust* (westernvirginialandtrust.org): Provide funds to preserve key tracts of land along the Parkway and seek private landowner support.

Blue Ridge Parkway: The Basics

History and Facts

Established: September 11, 1935

Visitors: About 16 million annually; ranks number one in visitation rates in the national park system

Designations: National Scenic Byway, All-American Road

Natural Heritage Areas: 47

States: Virginia and North Carolina

Time zone: Eastern time (ET)

Official website: www.nps.gov/blri

Physical Features

Acreage: 81,785 and 2,776 scenic easements

Elevation: Lowest point: 649.4 feet at James River in Virginia; highest point: 6,047 feet at Richland Balsam in North Carolina; peaks above 5,000 feet: 16

Mountain ranges: 5 in the central and southern Appalachians: Blue Ridge, Black, Pisgah, Balsam, Plott Balsam

National forests crossed: 4: George Washington, Jefferson, Nantahala, Pisgah

Water resources: 13 lakes; 3 major rivers: James, Roanoke, French Broad; 600 miles of streams; 115 headwaters; 15 watersheds

Average annual precipitation: Ranges from 41.4 inches at Roanoke, Virginia, to 48.1 inches at Asheville, North Carolina

Temperature range (F): Ranges from −17°F in Asheville, North Carolina, to 105°F in Roanoke, Virginia

Plant species: 2,074 species of vascular plants: species of wildflowers, trees and shrubs, grasses, sedges, ferns, fern allies

Plant communities: 75: 24 considered globally rare and 7 of these considered globally imperiled

Animal species: About 320 birds, 72 mammals,101 fish, 41 reptiles, 58 amphibians, unknown number of invertebrates

Rare species: 74 globally rare (G1-G3), 9 federally Threatened and Endangered species; 14 species of concern

Facilities

Entrances: Begin at Milepost 0 at the south end of Shenandoah National Park in Waynesboro, Virginia, end at Milepost 469 at the eastern entrance to Great Smoky Mountains National Park in Cherokee, North Carolina

Visitor centers: There are 15: Humpback Rocks at Milepost 5.8; James River at Milepost 63.6; Peaks of Otter at Milepost 85.9; Explore Park Visitor Center at Milepost 115; Rocky Knob at Milepost 169; Blue Ridge Music Center at Milepost 213; Moses Cone Park at Milepost 294.1; Linn Cove Viaduct at Milepost 304.4; Linville Falls at Milepost 316.4; Minerals Museum at Milepost 331; Crabtree Falls at Milepost 339.5; Craggy Gardens at Milepost 364.6; Folk Art Center at Milepost 382; Parkway Visitor Center at Milepost 384; Waterrock Knob at Milepost 451.2

Roads: 558 miles; 469 miles of scenic road

State secondary road accesses: 199: 104 in Virginia; 95 in North Carolina

Tunnels: 26; 1 in Virginia, 25 in North Carolina

Overlooks: 382: 281 scenic overlooks, 101 parking areas

Roadside vistas: 910 maintained

Views: 1,228

Miles of boundary: 1,200

Adjacent private landowners: More than 4,000; 101 private road accesses

Trails: 369 miles of trails including portions of the Appalachian National Scenic Trail and Mountains-to-Sea Trail

Campgrounds: 9 (1,037 sites): Otter Creek at Milepost 60.8; Peaks of Otter at Milepost 86; Roanoke Mountain at Milepost 120.4; Rocky Knob at Milepost 167.1 or 169; Doughton Park at Milepost 239.2 or 241.1; Julian Price Memorial Park at Milepost 297.1; Linville Falls at Milepost 316.4; Crabtree Falls at Milepost 339.5; Mount Pisgah at Milepost 408.6

Picnic areas: 13: Humpback Rocks at Milepost 5.8; James River at Milepost 63.8; Peaks of Otter at Milepost 86; Smart View at Milepost 154.5; Rocky Knob at Milepost 169; Cumberland Knob at Milepost 217.5; Doughton Park at Milepost 241.1; E. B. Jeffress Park at Milepost 272; Julian Price Memorial Park at Milepost 297.1; Linville Falls at Milepost 316.4; Crabtree Falls at Milepost 339.5; Craggy Gardens at Milepost 364.6; Mount Pisgah at Milepost 408.6. Also, many Parkway overlooks have picnic tables.

Lodging: 2: Peaks of Otter at Milepost 86; Mount Pisgah at Milepost 408.6. Check the Parkway website for current availability of other lodgings at www.nps.gov/blri/plany-ourvisit/lodging.htm.

Food: Peaks of Otter at Milepost 86; Mabry Mill at Milepost 176.1; Mount Pisgah at Milepost 408.6. Check Parkway website for current availability of dining at Doughton Park Milepost 241.1.

Fuel: Gasoline is not available on the Parkway but can be found in many nearby towns.

In May and June, breathtakingly beautiful displays of Catawba rhododendron line the Parkway.

Introduction

Endless waves of soft-blue mountaintops cradle the winding highway known as the Blue Ridge Parkway. Weaving its way through verdant Appalachian forests, the Blue Ridge Parkway rolls gracefully south for 469 matchless miles connecting Shenandoah National Park with its southern sister park, Great Smoky Mountains National Park. Once resembling the Himalayas, the Appalachians are an ancient landform, one of the oldest mountain ranges in the world. Over time, wind and water have softened the towering jagged mountains into endless pageants of waving, rolling crests that sweep into yawning valleys and flower-filled meadows. The sinuous backbone of the ancient Appalachians, the Blue Ridge Mountains stretch through the eastern states from southeastern Canada to Alabama. Untouched by the glaciers of the last ice age, the moderate climate and mild temperatures surrounding the Parkway, as it is fondly called, have created one of the most biologically diverse temperate areas in the world.

Nature Guide to the Blue Ridge Parkway is an easy-to-use pocket-size field guide to help visitors identify some of the most common plants, animals, and natural features of the area. Technical terms have been kept to a minimum, and color pictures accompany the descriptions. Perfectly sized to fit easily into a day pack, this compact field guide is filled with interesting information about each organism,

Early pioneers used the resources of nature to make needed items such as brooms.

The hike to Crabtree Falls is popular with Parkway visitors.

including natural history and ethnobotanical notes and other historical remarks. We care for the things that we know. Intended as an introduction to the nature of the Parkway, this small book will hopefully spark an interest in the natural world and generate further interest in caring for and supporting the environment. You can refer to the References section at the end of this book for further information and in-depth identification purposes.

About the Blue Ridge Parkway and Its Nature

A celebrated destination, the Blue Ridge Parkway beckons visitors from around the world to its magnificent vistas, cascading waterfalls, and cool mountain streams. Ranking number one in visitation rates in the National Park System, about 16 million people enjoy the Parkway annually.

Designated as a National Scenic Byway and an All-American Road in 2005, the Blue Ridge Parkway is managed by the National Park System. With a maximum speed limit of 45 and an average highway speed of 35 mph, motorists enjoy a journey on a road that is longer than the entire state of Florida. Spanning two states—Virginia and North Carolina—the Parkway passes through five mountain ranges and four national forests. It is no surprise that wildlife is plentiful and scenery is magnificent here.

To help the country recover from the financial devastation of the Great Depression, President Franklin D. Roosevelt spearheaded many public works projects, including the construction of a roadway that would connect Shenandoah National Park with Great Smoky Mountains National Park. Construction began in 1935 and provided much-needed income for many families. The Parkway is enjoyed by motorists as a route through the Blue Ridge Mountains, with well-planned scenic pullovers overlooking wide valleys and rolling mountains. The Parkway wasn't actually finished until 1987, with the completion of the Linn Cove Viaduct, an engineering marvel that was built around the S curves of Grandfather Mountain to preserve the fragile habitat. Planned as a slow-paced "drive for a while, stop for a while" recreational road, the Parkway allows visitors a unique view into the life of the Blue

Step back in time at Humpback Rocks Appalachian farm and cabin.

Ridge Mountains that would otherwise be inaccessible to motor vehicles. Many of the early pioneer structures have been remodeled or re-created along with displays and exhibits to help explain the culture of mountain life.

It is highly recommended that you stop early and often at Parkway Visitor Centers for helpful information to enhance your trip. The park personnel at the fifteen Visitor Centers along the Parkway can provide you with a map of the Parkway and let you know about local activities and events in their areas.

Make sure to ask about the Junior Ranger Program, which is available for anyone interested in learning more about this fantastic national treasure.

Along the roadway you will notice numbered mileposts that begin with zero at Rockfish Gap near Waynesboro, Virginia, and end at 469 near Cherokee, North Carolina. There is no entrance fee to the Blue Ridge Parkway, and although the Parkway is open year-round, most of the visitor services are only available from mid-May to late October or early November (services such as campgrounds and visitor centers are closed on a staggered basis).

Some sections of the Parkway's motor road may temporarily close in winter. You can check road closures at the Parkway's information line at (828) 298-0398 or on its website at www.nps.gov/blri. At a maximum speed limit of 45 mph, theoretically you could drive the 469 miles in about 11 hours, but due to the mountainous terrain, slow-moving vehicles, construction, wildlife, and safety concerns, you should allow for about 30 mph when figuring your actual travel time.

Optimally, you should allow at least four days of leisurely travel time to enjoy the scenic beauty of this exquisite land. The journey requires some planning as there is no fuel available on the Parkway and food and lodging are limited. Most visitors plan their trip with food stops and lodging reservations off the Parkway in the local towns bordering the road. See "Mileposts of Common Destinations on or near the Parkway" (page xviii) for help with planning your visit. The Blue Ridge Parkway Association publishes a helpful online directory for assistance with trip planning and gas station locations (blueridgeparkway.org). On the Parkway there are twenty-five tunnels in North Carolina and one in Virginia, some of which may limit the ability of large

The Parkway passes through twenty-six mountain tunnels.

motor homes to pass. Check the Parkway's website (www.nps.gov/blri/planyourvisit/tunnel-heights.htm) for more information as you are planning your trip.

The Parkway comes to life in springtime with colorful wildflowers and dazzling butterflies. Mid-June brings fantastic rhododendron blooms that cover the roadway and trails in a canopy of pink.

In autumn the surrounding communities attract avid leaf peepers who have come to the mountains to savor the glorious fall show of leaves. A haven for birds, fall visitors can turn their binoculars toward the sky to watch the migratory procession of warblers and hawks on their way to warmer climates. Taking great pictures is easy along the Parkway as photographers find enchanting subjects at every turn. Hundreds of trails are available, from easy leg-stretchers for time-pressed visitors to the Mountains-to-Sea Trail and the Appalachian Trail, which challenge marathon hikers. Waterfalls are on the must-see list for many Parkway visitors, and fortunately there are many to choose from, including Crabtree, Linville, and the falls at Graveyard Fields.

Mileposts of Common Destinations on or near the Parkway

Most visitor services on the Parkway are available mid-May through late October or early November. Camping reservations for some campgrounds on the Parkway may be reserved at www.recreation.gov or by calling (877) 444-6777. All others are available on a first-come, first-served basis. There is no fuel available on the Parkway, but fuel and other services may be found at many towns just off the Parkway. Note that there may be lengthy distances between fuel stops and plan accordingly.

Note: In the following section, MP = Milepost on the Blue Ridge Parkway. Bold print denotes destinations on the Blue Ridge Parkway. Restrooms are located at visitor centers and at most picnic areas.

MP Virginia

0.0   **Rockfish Gap**—north entrance to Blue Ridge Parkway
Waynesboro—4 miles west on US 250; lodging, food, fuel
Shenandoah National Park south entrance; nps.gov/shen

5.8   **Humpback Rocks**—visitor center, exhibits, picnic area, hiking, 1890s era Mountain Farm

13.7   Wintergreen Resort—1 mile east on VA 664; lodging, food, fuel, nature center, fishing, hiking; wintergreenresort.com

16.0   Sherando Lake Recreation Area, VA 814; George Washington National Forest, campground, swimming, boating, fishing

45.6   Buena Vista—5 miles west on US 60; lodging, food, fuel
Lexington—11 miles west on US 60; lodging, food, fuel

60.9   **Otter Creek**—campground, fishing, hiking

61.6   Natural Bridge—15 miles west on US 501; National Historic Landmark; lodging, food, fuel; naturalbridgeva.com

63.6   Lynchburg—22 miles east on US 501; lodging, food, fuel
James River—visitor center, picnic, fishing, hiking, restored canal locks

83.5   **Fallingwater Cascades**—hiking, waterfall

85.9   **Peaks of Otter**—visitor center, exhibits, nature center, lodging, food, picnic, campground, gift store, fishing, hiking, 1930s era historic Johnson Farm; Peaks of Otter Lodge, (540) 586-1081, peaksofotter.com

115.1   **Virginia's Explore Park**—visitor center, hiking, mountain biking trails (Check park website for available visitor services.)

120.4   Roanoke—lodging, food, fuel, hospital, all services; 105.8 US 460, 112.2 VA 24; 120.4 Mill Mountain Spur Road, 121.4 US 220
Roanoke Mountain—campground, hiking
Mill Mountain Discovery Center and Zoo, http://mmzoo.org

154.4   **Smart View**—picnic, hiking

169.0   **Rocky Knob**—visitor center, lodging, picnic, hiking

Traditional sounds of Appalachian music resound at the Blue Ridge Music Center.

Safety Notes

The driving experience on the Blue Ridge Parkway is uniquely designed to afford motorists with spectacular views that follow the natural flow of the mountains. The Parkway speed limit is generally 45 mph, but in some areas it drops to 25 mph or less. There are some steep grades and many winding curves, some with very limited sight distances. There are tight spiral curves in some places and areas with narrow shoulders—motorists should slow down in these areas. When passing through one of the twenty-six tunnels on the Parkway, turn on your headlights and watch for cyclists in the tunnel. The Parkway is a favorite destination drive for bicyclists and motorcyclists. Be sure to watch out for them and give them plenty of space. Perhaps the greatest distractions are the magnificent views. Allow time to pull over and enjoy the scenery and remember that others may be distracted by the view and are not paying attention to the road. Also be aware that wildlife such as bears and deer may dash onto the road with little notice. Fog often envelops the roadway, especially at the higher elevations—motorists should slow down in foggy conditions. When it is snowy or icy, avoid the Parkway altogether.

Changing weather conditions require cautious driving.

Always let someone know when you go for a hike. Dress in layers and carry rain gear and plenty of water as weather conditions can change rapidly. Be aware of fast-moving streams and waterfalls. Falling trees and branches can present hazards. Dehydration and sunburn can be prevented by drinking plenty of water and applying sunscreen. Do not drink untreated water from springs or streams as the seemingly clean water may harbor parasites like *Giardia lamblia,* which causes severe diarrhea.

Never feed wildlife. Not only is it illegal, it endangers the welfare of the animal. Stay a safe distance from all wildlife. There are poisonous snakes (timber rattlesnakes and copperheads) along the Parkway; be careful where you place your hands and feet, especially when climbing on rocks or in shrubby areas. Although there are no grizzly bears in the park, black bears do reside in the park. Most will avoid you if they hear you coming. Avoid hiking alone and never let small children run ahead of you on trails. Keep them beside you and pick them up if a bear is encountered. Ticks and mosquitoes are common throughout the park so take precautions such as using insect repellent and tucking your pants into your socks to prevent bites that may result in Lyme disease or Rocky Mountain spotted fever.

Report emergencies such as accidents, uncontrolled fires, or other safety hazards by calling (800) PARK-WATCH (800-727-5928).

Conservation Note

Please leave wildflowers and other plants where they grow. When hiking stay on established trails and watch where you put your feet to avoid damaging plants. Especially in cliff areas, avoid trampling plants as some of them may only be able to exist in these special conditions. Along the Blue Ridge Parkway limited quantities of berries, fruits, and nuts may be gathered for personal consumption. Keep in mind that it is illegal to pick, dig, or damage any plant. It is also illegal to collect rocks or minerals. Please report any suspicious activity such as plant poaching to a park ranger.

How to Use This Guide

In an effort to create consistent communication worldwide, each organism has a Latin name, genus, and species that is unique to that organism. In this book common names of families are given with the scientific family name in parentheses. In many cases an organism may have many common names, often varying by locality. In addition, genetic research is rapidly discovering new inherent relationships and associations; therefore the taxonomic status of many organisms may change with the new information. In general, organisms are listed alphabetically by family.

Photo Tips

Sharp focus is the key to taking great nature photos. Overcast days offer nice soft lighting for wildflowers and animals. In deep shade increase the ISO or use a flash. Bright, sunny days create harsh shadows, and a flash is needed to add detail to the dark, shaded areas of the flower or to add a speck of light to the eye. Image stabilization capability will help stop camera motion. For more advanced camera systems, shooting close-ups at f16 with a flash will give more depth of field and stop motion. When taking wildflower photos, be careful not to trample other plants. Use a telephoto lens to zoom in on wildlife and keep the eye in focus. Never approach too closely just to get a picture. If your behavior changes the behavior of the animal, you are too close. A tripod is necessary for low-light conditions in the early morning or evening.

Suggested Nature Hikes and Wildlife Viewing Areas near the Blue Ridge Parkway

The following areas or trails are suggested for the general public and families who want to see wildlife, wildflowers, and other natural features of the Blue Ridge Parkway. The milepost (MP) is given from north to south along the Parkway. Some of the recommended trails are wheelchair accessible or accessible with assistance. Of course, the wild animals and plants of the park may not always be where expected, so it is a good idea to first stop at a visitor center

Photographers revel in the kaleidoscopic fall colors along the Parkway.

and check with a park ranger about recent sightings. To find other attractive hikes, consult a topographic map or hiking guides such as Randy Johnson's *Best Easy Day Hikes Blue Ridge Parkway* and *Hiking the Blue Ridge Parkway* (FalconGuides). These and other interpretive publications are offered in the visitor centers along the Parkway. Always maintain a safe distance from wildlife and never feed wildlife. Please do not pick any wildflowers or remove any natural objects from the park. Remember, you're more likely to see wild animals during the early morning and evening, when they're more active.

1. James River—MP 63.6. Offering an excellent example of a riparian (river's edge) habitat, at 649.4 feet above sea level, the James River area is the lowest elevation on the Parkway. From the James River Visitor Center, you can take a short stroll on the James River Canal Trail. On the footbridge that crosses the James River, watch for water-loving birds such as osprey, bald eagles, green herons, and great blue herons. Eastern bluebirds and phoebes frequent the picnic area, and cliff swallows nest under the bridge. From the bank or a canoe, licensed fishermen can try for bass, bluegill, and other sunfish. The self-guiding 0.5-mile Trail of Trees is a great place to learn to identify native southern Appalachian hardwoods, as many of the trees along the trail are labeled with their names and natural history information.

2. Peaks of Otter—MP 85.9. Home of the endemic Peaks of Otter salamander, this is one of the best areas along the Parkway to regularly see white-tailed deer as they graze in the meadows surrounding the Peaks of Otter Lodge. Abbott Lake is perfectly situated to reflect the pyramid-shaped peak of Sharp Top Mountain. In the early morning and late evening, watch for playful river otters and statue-like great blue herons fishing for their meals. Visitors can hike the vigorous trail or ride the shuttle bus, for a fee, to the top of Sharp Top for great views into the surrounding countryside. Keep your eyes peeled for black bears in the forest. From September to

mid-October during fall migration, the trees in the area are alive with warblers, including Blackburnians, black-throated greens, black-throated blues, chestnut-sideds, and Cape Mays. If you are lucky, you may catch large flocks of common nighthawks soaring into the dusk.

3. Mabry Mill—MP 176.2. The most photographed place in the park is also a great place to see a good selection of flora and fauna. A fantastic display of southern red trillium graces the accessible trail in April and May. In late May and early June, Catawba rhododendrons provide photographers a colorful addition to their pictures of the mill and pond. Other wildflowers that bloom throughout the season include violets, saxifrage, skunk cabbage, and tassel rue.

4. Doughton Park—MP 241.1. Near Laurel Springs, Doughton Park is a quiet area of the park filled with rolling meadows. It is a great place to view wildlife including white-tailed deer, wild turkey, raccoons, and foxes. The prairie-like area is filled with wildflowers including dense blazing star, butterfly milkweed, coreopsis, and thistles, all of which attract a myriad of butterflies. Birds in the area include chipping sparrows, field sparrows, and eastern phoebes and barn swallows that like to nest in the eaves of buildings.

5. Moses H. Cone Memorial Park—MP 292.8 to 295.5; Julian Price Memorial Park—MP 295.5 to 298.6. From reindeer lichen to dabbling ducks, these two adjacent areas expand access to a rich southern Appalachian forest with miles of hiking and horseback-riding trails. This gorgeous area, once the estate of textile entrepreneur Moses Cone, is enjoyed by many who hike the carriage trails through the woodlands and around Price Lake. The woods are filled with mushrooms such as the painted boletes, which are found growing under the white pines. Ducks, including mallards and pied billed grebes, can be seen paddling on the edges of the lake. Wood ducks are abundant at nearby Bass Lake.

6. Linville Falls—MP 316.4. Linville Falls is one of the most popular Parkway destinations, offering views of a spectacular 45-foot falls drop into the 1,500-foot deep Linville Gorge. The significant geology of the area thrills geologists who visit the area to see the three fault lines that come together here. The rock that caps the falls is billion-year-old cranberry gneiss. Along the trail to the falls, you can see Carolina rhododendron, Carolina hemlock, sourwood, Christmas ferns, and hay-scented ferns.

7. Crabtree Falls—MP 339.5 A popular hike to a beautiful waterfall, the trail to Crabtree Falls is lined with moisture-loving ferns such as cinnamon, interrupted, and New York ferns. Along the trail you can see a variety of trees including several species of oak: black, red, white, scarlet, and chestnut. In July rosebay or great rhododendrons display their large white blossoms. Mushrooms such as russulas, amanitas, and lactarius can be found on the forest floor. Flowers such as fire pink, showy orchis, large-flowered trillium, and Dutchman's pipe decorate the woodlands.

8. Craggy Gardens—MP 364.6. Each year the June blooms of native Catawba rhododendrons draw nature lovers to the celebrated Craggy Gardens area. Typically the second or third week in June is when you can find these pink beauties in full bloom. In addition to the amazing display, this area is also a great place to see black bears, squirrels, veery, hermit thrush, and juncos, and in the fall the open picnic area is a great spot to watch for migrating hawks.

9. Mount Pisgah—MP 408.6. This high-altitude habitat supports a unique and varied population of plants and animals that thrive in the cool temperatures. In the campground there is a bog supporting a variety of interesting plants including smooth alder, angelica, and mushrooms such as chanterelles. Appalachian juncos breed and raise their young here but may descend down the mountain in harsh winters. Other summer birds to look for are cedar waxwings, blue-headed

vireo, American redstart, black-throated blue warblers, and black-throated green warblers. Here, eastern chipmunks dart about and feed on the tasty flowers of leatherflower, *Clematis viorna*. Other mammals to watch for include black bears, coyotes, white-tailed deer, and eastern cottontails.

10. Heintooga Overlook Spur Road—MP 458.2. A pleasant jaunt off the Parkway offers great possibilities for spying numerous bird species including hooded warblers, ovenbirds, downy and hairy woodpeckers, indigo buntings, and scarlet tanagers. Late-summer butterflies include great spangled fritillaries, skippers, and monarchs, while gray squirrels scamper among the oak, hickory, and sassafras trees. Black bears are sometimes seen here, and with the close proximity to Great Smoky Mountains National Park, there is also a possibility of spotting elk that wander into the Parkway from their park home in nearby Cataloochee Valley.

Designated as a National Recreation Trail in 2005, the Mountains-to-Sea Trail is one of the many hiking options for Parkway visitors.

ECOSYSTEMS

Following the Blue Ridge Mountains for 469 miles, the Parkway passes through five mountain ranges in the central and southern Appalachians and four national forests. As the longest continuous route into the Appalachian Mountains, the Parkway plays a major role in the protection of some of the most biologically diverse habitats in the United States. With an elevation range from roughly 650 feet at the James River to 6,047 feet at Richland Balsam, the diversity of flora and fauna is exceptional. More than 2,074 species of vascular plants have been identified here including 24 that are considered globally rare and 7 that are globally imperiled. Hundreds of species of animals call the Parkway home, with 74 listed as globally rare and 9 listed as threatened and endangered.

The climate of the southern Appalachian region is cool and wet, providing an ideal climate for organisms such as salamanders, millipedes, and fungi. About 11,000 years ago glaciers covered land as close as Pennsylvania to the north but didn't reach Virginia or North Carolina. Some of the northern species that were forced south still remain in the Blue Ridge on the high, cool mountain peaks. Minute genetic changes in these isolated populations, called relics, eventually result in species diversification.

A red squirrel relies on the cones of the high altitude red spruce tree.

The forest types of the Blue Ridge range from the drier oak-hickories in the northern section to the lush cove forests of magnolias and tulip trees in the central section. The southern-most section in the high elevations of the Balsam Mountains is characterized by dark-green spruce and fir trees. The trees release isoprene, which causes the bluish haze on the mountains that engendered the name Blue Ridge Mountains.

GEOLOGY

A series of events including continental landmass collisions and separations between North America and Africa, oceans forming and disappearing, and volcanic activity that occurred over the last 1.2 billion years all played a part in forming the tall peaks of the Appalachian Mountains that run from Canada to Georgia. Wind and water have slowly eroded the tall peaks that once resembled the rugged Rocky Mountains into the soft rolling Blue Ridge Mountains that we see today. Rocks called gneiss and granite make up most of the park's rock types and are evident in many of the overlooks and waterfalls. Areas in North Carolina are abundant in minerals, especially near Franklin and Spruce Pine, where there are several privately owned mines at which visitors can try their hand at gem mining.

COYOTE
Canis latrans
Dog family (Canidae)
Quick ID: medium size, doglike; gray to reddish coat; pointed, erect ears; long, slender snout; black-tipped tail usually carried straight down
Length: 2.5'–3.3' Weight: 15–44 lbs.

When natural balances are disrupted, nature has a way of filling in the gaps. In the East the extermination of top predators such as wolves and cougars has made ecological niches available for the adaptable coyote, which has expanded its range from the western states. Along the Parkway and in every county in Virginia and North Carolina, the coyote now takes its place as one of the top predators along with black bears and bobcats. This hardy and adaptable canine feeds mainly on small mammals such as mice, squirrels, and rabbits and will also take advantage of carrion, especially dead animals on the road. True omnivores, they will also supplement their diet with plant materials, including fruits such as apples and strawberries.

1

GRAY FOX
Urocyon cinereoargenteus
Dog family (Canidae)
Quick ID: salt-and-pepper grizzled gray back, dark streak on back and tail, black-tipped tail, rusty side, neck, legs, and feet
Length: 21"–29" Weight: 7–13 lbs.

Even though a gray fox has a grizzled gray upper coat, it has a rusty-reddish coloration on the sides of its neck, sides, and legs, often causing it to be misidentified as a red fox. The gray fox is slightly smaller than the red fox and has a fluffy 11- to 16-inch-long black-tipped tail rather than the white-tipped tail of the red fox. About the size of a miniature poodle, this small fox is the only member of the dog family that can climb trees. They make use of retractable claws to climb into trees to escape danger and to forage for fruits that make up a large part of their diet.

RED FOX
Vulpes vulpes
Dog family (Canidae)
Quick ID: small, doglike; reddish coat, white underneath; white-tipped, bushy tail
Length: 2.7'–3.6' Weight: 7–15 lbs.

Both admired and loathed, the red fox has charmed its way into folktales and legends as a cunning bandit whose sly character outwits both predator and prey. Using their keen eyesight, hearing, and sense of smell, foxes usually hunt in the late evening and early morning hours. As opportunistic omnivores, foxes will eat small mammals, birds, insects, plants, and berries. When food is abundant, they often kill more than they can eat and cache the surplus under leaves or bury it for leaner times. Along the Blue Ridge, farmers sometimes lost their entire flocks of chickens to the overambitious raid of a clever fox. Foxes were trapped or hunted, and their silky red pelts were sold or traded for supplies.

AMERICAN BEAVER
Castor canadensis
Beaver family (Castoridae)
Quick ID: dark-brown fur; broad, flat tail; short, round ears; webbed hind feet
Length: 3'–3.9' Weight: 35–66 lbs.

Remarkable wetland engineers, beavers build dams that not only provide shelter for their family colony of about 5 to 7 members, they are also keystone species that increase the biodiversity of their habitat. Many species of plants and animals benefit from wetland habitats including waterfowl, fish, amphibians, and reptiles such as the bog turtle, one of the rarest freshwater turtles in North America. Highly prized for their pelts for making clothing and top hats, beavers were once heavily trapped, and by the late 1800s they had become extinct in many states. Successful reintroduction programs are restoring populations of this important species along the Parkway. Mainly nocturnal, beavers may be seen at dusk at Price Lake, Bass Lake, and Otter Creek.

ELK
Cervus elaphus
Deer family (Cervidae)
Quick ID: larger than white-tailed deer, brown with large cream-colored rump patch
Length: 6.5'–8.5' Weight: 400–1,100 lbs.

By the late 1800s overhunting and loss of habitat eliminated elk from the southern Appalachians. In 2001 the resonating bugle of bull elks was once again heard in the region when a small herd was reintroduced into the Cataloochee Valley of Great Smoky Mountains National Park just south of the Blue Ridge Parkway. In North America moose are the largest member of the deer family, with elk in second place. Native Americans hunted elk for meat and fashioned their hides into clothing, shelter, laces, rope, and drumheads. The successful reintroduction program in the Smokies will help this vanished species freely roam the mountains as they did before European settlement. Keep an eye out for elk along the Heintooga Spur Road.

WHITE-TAILED DEER
Odocoileus virginianus
Deer family (Cervidae)
Quick ID: reddish-tan in summer, grayish-brown in winter; white around eyes and nose; white throat, stomach, and underside of tail; males have antlers, females without antlers
Length: 3'–7.8' Weight: 147–297 lbs.

One of the most commonly seen wild animals along the Parkway, white-tailed deer can be seen grazing in meadows and fields and along road-sides, especially in open areas such as Peaks of Otter and Doughton Park. During the autumn rutting season, bucks display their proud antlers as they wrestle over the right to mate with a doe. The size and number of points of a buck's antlers is determined by genetics, diet, and health as well as age, with most males reaching their prime at about 6 years. Growing as much as 0.5 inch per day, the bony antlers are shed in winter. To avoid an accident, please be vigilant of these and other animals crossing the road, especially at night.

DEER MOUSE
Peromyscus maniculatus
Mice, rat, and vole family (Cricetidae)
Quick ID: grayish to reddish brown, white underparts, white feet, long bicolored tail, large beady eyes, large round ears
Length: 2.8"–4", tail: 2"–5" Weight: 0.66–1.25 oz.

A close relative of the white-footed mouse, *P. leucopus,* the deer mouse has a long bicolored tail with a very clear delineation between the brown upper part and the lower white part. These and other mice nest under logs and stones and in tree cavities. Deer mice can produce from 2 to 4 litters per year, typically with 3 to 5 young. The young are born blind and helpless but grow rapidly and are capable of breeding about 49 days later. An important foundation in the ecological food chain, these and other rodents are an important source of protein for a wide variety of predators including hawks, owls, foxes, skunks, raccoons, and snakes.

MUSKRAT
Ondatra zibethicus
Mice, rat, and vole family (Cricetidae)
Quick ID: brown, laterally flattened tail, aquatic
Length: 16"–24" Weight: 1.5–3.9 lbs.

Found in marshy areas, ponds, streams, and wetlands, the muskrat has webbed hind feet and a rudder-like tail that helps it maneuver through its habitat. Aptly named for the strong musky odor produced, muskrats mark their territories using their scent glands. Although they are considered a valuable species in the fur trade, populations remain stable due to their high reproductive rate, producing 2 to 3 litters of young per year. They can remain underwater for up to 17 minutes while swimming 100 yards. They feed primarily on aquatic plants, especially cattails and rushes, but they will also eat frogs, crayfish, and fish.

PINE VOLE
Microtus pinetorum
Mice, rat and vole family (Cricetidae)
Quick ID: chestnut-brown fur, buffy below; short 1" tail; small ears and eyes
Length: 2.8"–4.2" Weight: 0.75–1.33 oz.

Pine or woodland voles occur throughout most of the eastern United States. While the genus name, *Microtus,* referring to small ears, is appropriate, the species name, *pinetorum,* is somewhat misleading, as this vole actually prefers deciduous woods with thick leaf litter rather than pine forests. These voles share the same habitat with deer and white-footed mice, jumping mice, moles, and shrews. They dig shallow tunnels that connect underground chambers in which they cache food for the winter. Farmers and orchardists consider pine voles to be pests as they can damage crops, especially apple trees, potatoes, peanuts, and planted seeds. Primary predators are foxes, snakes, hawks, and owls.

VIRGINIA OPOSSUM
Didelphis virginiana
Opossum family (Didelphidae)
Quick ID: grizzled gray, white face, pointed snout, pink-tipped black ears, long hairless tail
Length: 15"–20"   Weight: 9–13 lbs.

Belonging to the same class of animals as kangaroos and koalas, the Virginia opossum is the only marsupial found north of Mexico. More than 100 species of opossums live in South America, ranging from the size of a mouse to that of a cat. The largest member, the Virginia opossum, has extended its range northward through Central America, Mexico, and recently into Canada. Active throughout the year, the freezing temperatures of northern winters may result in frostbitten ears and tails. Opossums are omnivores, eating a wide variety of foods including fruits, grains, insects, and carrion. Considered a delicacy, opossums were frequently hunted, skinned, and then roasted with sweet potatoes or turnip greens.

BOBCAT
Lynx rufus
Cat family (Felidae)
Quick ID: tawny to gray with black spots and bars, black ear tufts, short tail
Length: 1.5'–4' Weight: 8.4–68 lbs.

Although they are abundant in the Blue Ridge Mountains, bobcats are rarely seen by visitors. Secretive and silent hunters, the primary prey of the bobcat are rabbits and mice. Bobcats are crepuscular animals, active during dawn and dusk. While resting and sleeping they seek shelter in hollow trees, rock piles, and brush piles. Solitary animals, bobcats communicate their territory by scent marking and scratching a tree or log that leaves a mark and scent. During mating season their plaintive calls can be heard echoing through the hollows and across mountaintops, resounding in the eerie darkness and reminding listeners that the wilderness is still alive along the Parkway.

EASTERN COTTONTAIL
Sylvilagus floridanus
Rabbit family (Leporidae)
Quick ID: rusty gray-brown fur, underside fur white; large hind feet; long ears; short, fluffy white tail; rusty patch on nape of neck
Length: 14"–17"   Weight: 2–4 lbs.

The eastern cottontail is a very prolific species: A single female, called a doe, averages 3 to 4 litters a year. With about 5 kits per litter, a buck (male cottontail) and a doe could produce 25 rabbits a year. This elevated reproductive rate is needed to offset the high predation rate as cottontails play a substantial role in sustaining many other inhabitants of the forest. Predators include foxes, bobcats, owls, and hawks. Mountain settlers also relied on the cottontail as a food source and for warm clothing. The rare Appalachian cottontail may be found in dense conifer forests at upper elevations. It is slightly smaller than the eastern cottontail and has a dark patch between the ears.

STRIPED SKUNK
Mephitis mephitis
Skunk family (Mephitidae)
Quick ID: black, 2 broad white stripes along back, large bushy tail
Length: 20"–2.3' Weight: 6–14 lbs.

With the descriptive Latin name *Mephitis* meaning "foul gas or bad odor," the skunk is well named. Commonly called "polecat," the word *skunk* is derived from the Algonquin word *seganku,* meaning "one who squirts." When threatened these masters of chemical defense spew a stream of foul-smelling oily liquid a distance of up to 10 to feet away, causing burning of the eyes and nose and nausea for the unfortunate victim. Contrary to popular belief, tomato juice only masks the odor. A mixture of 3 percent hydrogen peroxide, a quarter cup of baking soda, and some liquid dishwashing soap provides effective relief but may change hair color. The smaller eastern spotted skunk is also found in the park.

NORTHERN RIVER OTTER
Lontra canadensis
Weasel family (Mustelidae)
Quick ID: rich brown fur; long, round tail; webbed feet
Length: 2.9'–4.3' Weight: 11–30 lbs.

With its streamlined but powerful body, webbed feet, and rudder-like tail, the river otter is well adapted for a semiaquatic habitat. Underwater they launch torpedo-like attacks on fish such as carp, perch, and sunfish. Hunting primarily at night, they use their sensitive whiskers as feelers to prey on frogs, crayfish, and insects. Heavily trapped for their thick, rich fur, the northern river otter was extirpated (became extinct) in certain areas of the country, including parts of Virginia and western North Carolina. Reintroduction and conservation efforts have produced a growing population. A great place to see otters is Abbot Lake at Peaks of Otter, where they live and play under the shadow of Sharp Top Mountain.

RACCOON
Procyon lotor
Raccoon family (Procyonidae)
Quick ID: grizzled brownish gray, stocky body, pointed snout, black facial mask, 5–7 black rings on bushy 8"–12"-long tail
Length: 18"–28" Weight: 4–23 lbs.

Endearing to nature lovers but at times despised by homeowners, raccoons are well known for their resolute persistence in obtaining what they want. The black "bandit" mask around their eyes helps camouflage them during their nightly forages for wild foods, which include fruits, nuts, insects, rodents, and fish. With a magician's ability to open seemingly impenetrable locks, the nimble-fingered raccoon soon makes enemies of farmers who lose stored crops such as corn, apples, and even chickens. For residents, a good coonhound was one of their most prized possessions as a carefully prepared raccoon pelt could be sold to make coonskin fur coats and "Daniel Boone"-style caps that provided extra income. Coonhounds are still kept and used for hunting, but coonskin isn't so popular anymore.

EASTERN CHIPMUNK
Tamias striatus
Squirrel family (Sciuridae)
Quick ID: small, reddish brown; one white stripe on each side bordered by black; creamy white broken eye ring
Length: 5"–6" Weight: 2.5–4.5 oz.

The eastern chipmunk is the sole species of chipmunk in the eastern states, whereas wildlife lovers in the West are challenged with identifying numerous species of chipmunks. Chipmunks are most active in the afternoon when shadows blend with the stripes on their backs to help them remain camouflaged from aerial predators such as hawks and ravens. Chipmunks excavate an extensive network of tunnels that lead to a nest about 3 feet below the ground surface. During the winter they remain in their underground burrows in a state of torpor, rousing about twice a week to eat from their supply of stored nuts and seeds.

GRAY SQUIRREL
Sciurus carolinensis
Squirrel family (Sciuridae)
Quick ID: salt-and-pepper gray back and bushy tail, brown sides, white underparts
Length: body 8"–10", tail 8"–10"   Weight: 9–17 oz.

With a fluffy tail as long as its head and body, the eastern gray squirrel has a total length of about 20 inches. The genus name *Sciurus* means "tail shadow," referring to the ability of a squirrel to sit in the shadow of its own luxuriant tail. Male and female gray squirrels are similar in size and coloration, but some melanistic individuals are totally black. Squirrels provided an important source of food for Native Americans and settlers, with squirrel stew making it to the list of favorite meals of President Andrew Jackson. Except in national parks, where hunting is illegal, this animal is currently one of the most important game species in the country, with an annual harvest of about 40 million.

WOODCHUCK
Marmota monax
Squirrel family (Sciuridae)
Quick ID: brownish-gray, heavy body; short legs; tail about 5"
Length: 16"–20" Weight: 5–10 lbs.

One of the most frequently seen animals along the Blue Ridge Parkway, the woodchuck, or groundhog, is the honorary mascot of the area. With strong limbs and sharp, curved claws, groundhogs dig 4- to 5-foot-deep underground burrows that are 14 to 30 feet long. Like their western marmot cousins, they hibernate in burrows from November to February. When alarmed they sound a shrill whistle before scampering to safety, inspiring the nickname "whistlepig." Prodigious eaters, a groundhog may consume more than ⅓ of its body weight per day feasting on grasses, leaves, and crops. Groundhog hunting once ridded farmlands of these "pests." The meat was roasted in stews and the prepared hides were used as banjo heads.

BLACK BEAR
Ursus americanus
Bear family (Ursidae)
Quick ID: large; black; round ears; flat-footed walk
Length: 4'–6.5' Weight: 86–900 lbs.

An iconic symbol of the American wilderness, many visitors to the Parkway come with high hopes of seeing a black bear in the wild. Primarily vegetarians, black bears forage throughout the Parkway on foods such as grass, fruits, and acorns. In autumn they may consume up to 20,000 calories per day to prepare for their long winter slumber in rock caves, hollow trees, or brush thickets. Unfortunately, some bears have become habituated to humans and have discovered that garbage and even picnics can provide an easy food source. These problem bears pose a risk for visitors to the Parkway and often have to be destroyed. Please make sure to keep your food secured in a bear-proof container.

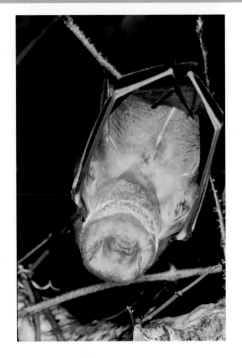

RED BAT
Lasiurus borealis
Bat family (Vespertilionidae)
Quick ID: males—bright red, females—dull red; both frosted white on back and breast with white patch on shoulders
Length: 3.7"–4.4" Weight: 0.25–0.5 oz.

Slicing through the evening sky, the nightly flight of bats begins at dusk as their pinpoint echolocation zeros in on insects such as moths, mosquitoes, and flies. Bats are often seen zipping around headlights or light posts, which attract insects. Many bats, such as the red bat, roost in trees during the day. In fall they migrate south for the winter, unlike other species, such as the little brown bat, that winter in caves. It is these cave-roosting bats that have been subject to a devastating fungal disease called white-nose syndrome that is decimating their numbers in its path.

BROAD-WINGED HAWK
Buteo platypterus
Diurnal raptor family (Accipitridae)
Quick ID: small hawk; rusty striped breast; light underwings; thick, black-and-white stripes on short tail
Length: 15" Weight: 14 oz. Wingspan: 34"

In great reunions broad-winged hawks gather together for the annual exodus from their summer mountain home to their southern wintering grounds in the tropics. Taking advantage of warm rising air currents, the hawks soar in huge tornado-like spirals known as kettles over the Blue Ridge Mountains. With binoculars trained on the skies, birders wait patiently each fall for the ageless spectacle of nature in migration. These enthusiastic nature lovers have discovered the thrill of spotting thousands of winged raptors following ancient highways through the clouds. In mid-September broad-wings can be seen at many open overlooks along Parkway ridges, especially Mount Pisgah, Mahogany Rocks, Harvey's Knob, and Rockfish Gap, where you can join skilled birders enjoying the annual air show.

RED-TAILED HAWK
Buteo jamaicensis
Diurnal raptor family (Accipitridae)
Quick ID: large, brown hawk; broad, rounded wings; broad, reddish tail; streaked bellyband
Length: 19" Weight: 2.4 lbs. Wingspan: 49"

The red-tailed hawk is the most common hawk in North America, however, they show extreme geographic variation in plumage. In the East red-tails have a rusty milk-chocolate-brown coloration, while their western counterparts can be dark chocolate to black with contrasting white markings. Red-tails have a dark bellyband formed by vertical streaks across the white belly. Red-shouldered hawks have red barring covering their belly and a distinctly barred tail. Broad-winged hawks are smaller with a distinctly barred tail. Other raptors to compare are bald and golden eagles, which are much larger, and northern harriers, with their long wings and tail. Other commonly seen hawks are Cooper's and sharp-shinned hawks, but both are much smaller than the red-tail.

WOOD DUCK
Aix sponsa
Duck, geese, swan family (Anatidae)
Quick ID: male—brightly colored chestnut and green, crested head with bold white striping patterns, red bill and eye; female—dull brownish gray, white eye ring
Length: 18.5" Weight: 1.3 lbs. Wingspan: 30"

The most distinctive and regal of all of the dabbling ducks, the male wood duck outshines all others. During breeding season males display their colorful plumage to attract females. Although most ducks nest on the ground, wood ducks nest in tree cavities, often over still or slow-moving water, where they lay about 10 eggs. About a day after hatching, at their mother's call the tiny baby ducks jump in a brave leap of faith from heights of up to 80 feet or more and, unharmed, they make their way to the water. Large flocks of wood ducks can be seen at Bass and Price Lakes.

GREAT BLUE HERON
Ardea herodias
Heron and egret family (Ardeidae)
Quick ID: tall; gray; long legs; long neck; long, heavy yellow bill
Length: 46" Weight: 5.3 lbs. Wingspan: 72"

The great blue heron is the largest member of its family in North America. These large blue-gray herons are often mistaken for cranes. Great blues fly with their necks curved into an S, while cranes, such as the sandhill crane found in western states, fly with their necks outstretched. Great blue herons are commonly found along rivers and ponds and will eat fish, frogs, and even small mammals. Patient feeders, they possess the ability to stand motionless until striking. In their graceful, slow flight, they trail their long legs behind them, sometimes uttering a loud guttural "raaaunk" call. Look for these herons at Abbot, Otter, Price, and Bass Lakes as well as along the James, Roanoke, and French Broad Rivers.

CEDAR WAXWING
Bombycilla cedrorum
Waxwing family (Bombycillidae)
Quick ID: grayish brown, crest on head, black mask edged with white, pale yellow on breast and belly, wings tipped red, yellow band on tail
Length: 7.25" Weight: 1.1 oz. Wingspan: 12"

With silky gray plumage offset by a yellow breast, pointed crest, and black mask, cedar waxwings are well outfitted to stand out in the bird world. But perhaps what makes these the favorite of many birders are the wings of the adults, which look like they were dipped in red wax. Traveling in small flocks, the yellow band on the end of the tail is often a good clue to help identify them as their quiet twitter is understated in the wild. Waxwings eat berries and other fruits and rely on the small blue cones of eastern red cedar in the winter, giving them their common name.

INDIGO BUNTING
Passerina cyanea
Cardinal family (Cardinalidae)
Quick ID: male—deep blue; female—light brown, faint streaking, pale throat
Length: 5.5" Weight: 0.51 oz. Wingspan: 8"

The spring arrival announcement of the indigo bunting is often heard as the musical twice-over song "here, here, where, where." The bright-blue males often perch on treetops or shrubs to proclaim their territories along forest edges and roadsides along the Parkway. The iridescent-blue feather coloration of the male is in stark contrast to the dull brown of the female. Males vie for the attention of several females, and the cobalt blue coloration helps them attract suitable mates. The dull-brown feathers of the female serve to conceal them during nesting season, thus helping to ensure proliferation of the species.

NORTHERN CARDINAL
Cardinalis cardinalis
Cardinal family (Cardinalidae)
Quick ID: large, orange-red bill ringed in black, crest on head, long tail; male—bright red;
female—buffy tan, red edging on wings
Length: 8.75" Weight: 1.6 oz. Wingspan: 12"

The northern cardinal is one of the most familiar birds of the eastern
and Midwestern states. The northern cardinal is the state bird of both
Virginia and North Carolina. A popular bird, it shares this honor with the
states of Indiana, Illinois, Kentucky, West Virginia, and Ohio. No other
bird comes close to this popularity ranking. The heavy bill is a good indi-
cation that cardinals are seed eaters, but they also supplement their diet
with fruits and insects. The Latin name, *Cardinalis cardinalis*, is derived
from the red color of the robes of Roman Catholic cardinals.

ROSE-BREASTED GROSBEAK
Pheucticus ludovicianus
Cardinal family (Cardinalidae)
Quick ID: large, conical, pale bill; male—black head and back, white markings, red triangle on breast, white underparts; female—coarse brown streaking overall, white eyebrow
Length: 8"   Weight: 1.6 oz.   Wingspan: 12.5"

Even with the strikingly bold color patterns of the male rose-breasted grosbeak, this songbird is sometimes difficult to see amidst the foliage. Singing sweetly from branches, their loud, melodic song may remind you of the sound of sneakers squeaking on a gym floor. The female resembles a large sparrow with dull brown streaks, perfect for camouflage to help protect her from predators while nesting. Grosbeaks have large, heavy bills, which enable them to eat a variety of insects and seeds. Look for grosbeaks along the Tanawha Trail near Grandfather Mountain, Craggy Gardens, and Mount Mitchell State Park.

TURKEY VULTURE
Cathartes aura
New World vulture family (Cathartidae)
Quick ID: black; silvery flight feathers; bare, red head; flies with wings in dihedral
Length: 26"   Weight: 4 lbs.   Wingspan: 67"

The eagle-size dark birds often seen soaring over the overlooks along the Parkway are often misidentified as buzzards. Turkey vultures and the related black vultures are also mistaken for hawks or eagles. Black vultures have pale areas at the end of their wings, and turkey vultures have pale silvery areas along the back portion of their outstretched wings. Black vultures fly with straight wings, while turkey vultures fly with their wings held in a shallow V shape called a dihedral. Turkey vultures often teeter from side to side, soaring on warm breezes as they search for food using an extremely heightened sense of smell to locate carrion. Vultures are important members of the ecosystem as scavengers.

BLUE JAY
Cyanocitta cristata
Crow family (Corvidae)
Quick ID: blue upperparts, blue crest, white marking on wings and tail, gray breast, black necklace
Length: 11" Weight: 3 oz. Wingspan: 16"

Blue jays and their cousins Steller's jays, which are found in western North America, are members of the crow family. These 2 jays sport a pointed crest of feathers on their heads that may be raised and lowered at will and is often used to intimidate rivals or predators. Jays are excellent mimics, and their calls and sounds can fool even the best birder. Blue jays will engage in mobbing behavior, harassing unwanted birds or even hawks that enter their territory. Similarly colored blue birds include the eastern bluebird and the indigo bunting, both about half the size of the blue jay. The eastern bluebird has a rosy breast and the solid-blue indigo bunting lacks the crest.

COMMON RAVEN
Corvus corax
Crow family (Corvidae)
Quick ID: large; solid black; long, narrow wings; wedge-shaped tail; heavy bill
Length: 24" Weight: 2.6 lbs. Wingspan: 53"

The object of lore and legend, common ravens have intrigued humans since ancient times. The largest member of the crow family, ravens are considered by researchers to be one of the most intelligent members of the avian world. They often perform elaborate aerial acrobatics, rolling in midflight and even flying upside down with ease. Both feared and worshipped, Native Americans believed that wild animals represented specific meanings in life, and many thought that all birds are messengers to the Great Spirit. Often confused with the crow, notice the big, thick bill and the wedge-shaped tail of the raven as opposed to the thin, short bill and rather squared-off tail of the crow.

CHIPPING SPARROW
Spizella passerina
Sparrow family (Emberizidae)
Quick ID: brown back with black streaks, rufous crown, white eyebrow, black eye stripe, grayish breast, grayish rump
Length: 5.5" Weight: 0.42 oz. Wingspan: 8.5"

Chipping sparrows are commonly seen along roadside edges and at overlooks along the Parkway. They often run on the ground to chase insects or hop up to feed on grass seeds. The bright rufous cap helps to identify this small sparrow, but birds less than a year old often have less distinctly marked striped rufous caps and are paler overall. Look for these small sparrows at Julian Price Memorial Park, Mount Pisgah, and Virginia's Explore Park.

DARK-EYED JUNCO
Junco hyemalis
Sparrow family (Emberizidae)
Quick ID: gray above, white belly, white outer tail feathers, conical bill
Length: 6.25" Weight: 0.67 oz. Wingspan: 9.25"

One of the most commonly encountered birds along the Parkway, juncos frequent the edges of parking lots and roadways. Their twittering trill is frequently heard, and they can sound a lot like a pine warbler or chipping sparrow. Two subspecies of juncos can be found along the Parkway. Juncos that are resident Appalachian Mountain birds year-round have bluish bills. In winter migrants from the northern states and Canada sporting pinkish bills join their numbers but return to the north in spring. Juncos often build a well-concealed nest on slopes, cliff faces, or on the ground. As they feed on insects or seeds, dark-eyed juncos tend to hop or walk on the ground.

33

EASTERN TOWHEE
Pipilo erythrophthalmus
Sparrow family (Emberizidae)
Quick ID: stocky sparrow, long tail, conical bill, rufous sides, white belly, red eye; male—black head and back; female—brown head and back
Length: 8.5" Weight: 1.4 oz. Wingspan: 10.5"

If you happen to hear something moving in the underbrush, it may be an eastern towhee scratching in the underbrush and tossing dead leaves aside in its search for insects. The eastern towhee is closely related to the spotted towhee found in western states, and until recently they were considered a single species called the rufous-sided towhee. The spotted towhee has white wing bars and spots on its back, both characteristics the eastern towhee lacks. The distinctive song of "drink your teeeeee" and a "chewink" call note are perhaps the best ways to find this bird as it is often hidden in the underbrush.

AMERICAN GOLDFINCH
Carduelis tristis
Finch family (Fringillidae)
Quick ID: short conical bill, short notched tail, white wing bars; male—yellow with black forehead, wings, and tail; female—dull, greenish yellow
Length: 5" Weight: 0.46 oz. Wingspan: 9"

The entertaining acrobats of the avian world, American goldfinches comically hang upside down from a tall thistle or flower head plucking seeds before quickly flitting away. As social birds, they often fly in small flocks with their characteristic bouncy undulating flight and their chipping "potato chip" call. Sometimes called "wild canaries," both males and females molt their bright yellow summer plumage into drab brown feathers that aid in camouflage during the winter months. The drab winter plumage sometimes is confused with that of the pine siskin, which is streaked with brown overall and has a more pointed bill. In summer the brightly colored yellow warbler can be seen, but it lacks the black markings of the goldfinch.

TREE SWALLOW
Tachycineta bicolor
Swallow family (Hirundinidae)
Quick ID: stocky, shiny blue-green upperparts, white throat and underparts, small bill
Length: 5.75" Weight: 0.7 oz. Wingspan: 14.5"

Entertaining visitors to the Parkway, tree swallows swoop and dive over ponds and lakes while catching insects in midair. They have been clocked flying at over 18 mph. Swallows nest in dead trees in vacant woodpecker holes or under the eaves of buildings, usually in open areas near water. In the fall swallows form large flocks at dusk and fly in dense clouds before settling into a tree for the evening. A much larger bird with the same shape as a swallow is the common nighthawk, which can be seen in migration soaring in large flocks. Look for tree swallows along the Parkway at Abbott, Price, and Bass Lakes.

BALTIMORE ORIOLE
Icterus galbula
Blackbird family (Icteridae)
Quick ID: White wing bars, sharp pointed bill; male—black and orange; female—grayish brown and yellow
Length: 8.75" Weight: 1.2 oz. Wingspan: 11.5"

The spectacular Baltimore oriole is one of the most colorful of the neotropical migrants that summer along the Blue Ridge Parkway. A bit smaller and slimmer than an American robin, the Baltimore oriole may be seen in open-area treetops whistling a flutelike song. The bright-orange and black plumage of the male happened to be the same colors as those on the coat of arms of Lord Baltimore, the first governor of the Maryland colony in the 1600s, hence the common name Baltimore oriole. Look for Baltimore orioles in deciduous open woods, especially along waterways such as the James and Roanoke Rivers.

GRAY CATBIRD
Dumetella carolinensis
Mimic-thrush family (Mimidae)
Quick ID: slate gray, black cap and tail, rufous undertail feathers (coverts)
Length: 8.5" Weight: 1.3 oz. Wingspan: 11"

The catlike "meeeurr" call of the gray catbird gives this species its name. The northern mockingbird and the brown thrasher are the other eastern members of the Mimid family. These birds forage on the ground for insects, using their bills to toss dead leaves aside. The northern mockingbird has white in the wings and tail with white underparts. The brown thrasher is brown with brown streaking on the underparts. Mockingbirds repeat their call phrases 3 times, the thrasher twice, and the catbird once. Gray catbird numbers are in decline in the southeastern United States due to habitat loss.

CAROLINA CHICKADEE
Poecile carolinensis
Chickadee and titmice family (Paridae)
Quick ID: black cap, black throat, white cheek, pale gray below, gray back, gray wings with narrow whitish edging, indistinct edge between white cheek and gray back
Length: 4.75" Weight: 0.37 oz. Wingspan: 7.5"

A firecracker in a small package, the tiny Carolina chickadee is nonstop action in the treetops. These black-and-white bundles of chattering feathers chime their name, "chick-a-dee-dee-dee" as they glean insects from leaves and bark. Their energetic actions delight birders as they fearlessly browse on insects and seeds in open wooded areas. Black-capped chickadees are found in high-elevation mountainous areas of the Parkway, especially where spruce and fir grow. Black-capped chickadees have lower-pitched call notes. They also sport a bright white "hockey stick" pattern on their wings and a distinct edge between the all-white cheek and gray back.

TUFTED TITMOUSE
Baeolophus bicolor
Chickadee and titmice family (Paridae)
Quick ID: blue-gray back and crest, black forehead, orange sides, white underparts, large black eyes
Length: 6.5" Weight: 0.75 oz. Wingspan: 9.75"

Campers along the Parkway often wake to the lilting "peter-peter-peter" song of the tufted titmouse in the morning air. Tufted titmice are common along the Parkway at low elevations, especially in areas near oak forests. Males and females look alike, with blue-gray upperparts and creamy-white underparts. When agitated, titmice raise their pointed crest and chatter angrily. Tufted titmice nest in tree holes and cavities left by woodpeckers and depend on dead and dying trees for these nest sites. They forage on insects, seeds, nuts, and berries. In winter they forage on seeds and acorns that they crack with their stout bill. Even though tufted titmice resemble energetic mice, the name titmouse means "small bird."

AMERICAN REDSTART
Setophaga ruticilla
Wood-warbler family (Parulidae)
Quick ID: male—black and orange; female—grayish and yellow
Length: 5.25" Weight: 0.29 oz. Wingspan: 7.75"

Flitting through vegetation while fanning its tail, the American redstart is a common warbler in spring and summer. The male redstart boasts Halloween colors of black and orange, while the female is dull grayish with yellow markings. These small songbirds are very active as they glean insects from the trees or catch them in flight in an aerial display called flycatching. Two warblers that are similar in appearance to the male American redstart are the Blackburnian warbler and the magnolia warbler. The Blackburnian lacks the orange in the wings and tail, and the magnolia has a yellow chest with dark markings and white spots in the tail rather than the yellow or orange patches in the tail.

41

BLACK-THROATED GREEN WARBLER
Dendroica virens
Wood-warbler family (Parulidae)
Quick ID: olive-green back, yellow face, 2 white wing bars, black streaks on sides, white outer tail feathers; male—black on throat and breast; female—whitish chin
Length: 5" Weight: 0.31 oz. Wingspan: 7.75"

The small warbler is one of the most common summer breeders along the Blue Ridge Parkway. Its bright yellow face, black bib, and green back are characteristic. Many warblers species show major differences in plumage between male and female. The male and female black-throated green warblers are similar in appearance but the female lacks the black bib of the male. In fall immature warblers and some adults display dull brown and pale yellow plumages and are often called confusing fall warblers among birders, but the white wing bars are helpful in identifying this species. Look for this and other warblers gleaning tree branches for insects in deciduous trees such as those at Peaks of Otter.

WILD TURKEY
Meleagris gallopavo
Upland game bird family (Phasianidae)
Quick ID: dark-brown body, unfeathered bluish head with red markings and wattles, brown tail with buffy tips
Length: 37"–46" Weight: 9–16 lbs. Wingspan: 50"–64"

One of the most frequently seen birds along the Blue Ridge Parkway is the wild turkey. Although not regarded as the most glamorous member of the avian world, turkeys have played an important role in our culture and society. Wild turkeys were an important source of food for Native Americans and early European settlers. Native Americans used turkey feathers as decorations, and they were woven into capes for use during the winter. Benjamin Franklin thought so much of the turkey that he favored it over the bald eagle as the patriotic symbol of the United States. Turkeys can be seen grazing in open fields and forest edges along the Parkway including Peaks of Otter, Love Gap, and Heintooga Spur Road.

RED-BELLIED WOODPECKER
Melanerpes carolinus
Woodpecker family (Picidae)

Quick ID: black-and-white barred back and wings, white rump, sharp chisel-like black bill, faint reddish belly; male—entire crown and nape red; female—grayish forehead, nape red

Length: 9.25"   Weight: 2.2 oz.   Wingspan: 16"

Perhaps a better name for the red-bellied woodpecker would be zebra-backed woodpecker as the black-and-white striped back is much easier to see than the faint red belly. Females have a pale forehead with a red patch on the back of the neck, while males have an entirely red crown and nape. They are sometimes mistaken for red-headed woodpeckers, which have an entirely red head and neck. Pileated woodpeckers are much larger with a large red crest. The hairy and the very common downy woodpeckers are both smaller than the red-bellied. Yellow-bellied sapsuckers have indistinct black-and-white back markings. Yellow-shafted flickers are brownish with black barring. Look for these and other woodpeckers throughout the Parkway.

YELLOW-BELLIED SAPSUCKER
Sphyrapicus varius
Woodpecker family (Picidae)
Quick ID: black back with faint white bars, black wings with white patch, white rump, red forehead, black line through eye, yellow belly with streaking on sides; male—red throat; female—white throat
Length: 8.5" Weight: 1.8 oz. Wingspan: 16"

A member of the woodpecker family, yellow-bellied sapsuckers are brightly colored with a red forehead, black back with faint bars, and a true-to-its-name yellow belly. White patches on the black wings help to identify it in its undulating flight. Sapsuckers make rows of horizontal holes in trees to get to the sap, which they lap up with their long, bristly tongues. Most sapsuckers breed in Canada and northern states, but at the higher elevations on the Blue Ridge, an Appalachian subspecies breeds in boreal forests. These Appalachian yellow-bellied sapsuckers are smaller and darker. You can look for these special woodpeckers at high elevations such as Richland Balsam trail and Black Balsam road.

RUBY-CROWNED KINGLET
Regulus calendula
Kinglet family (Regulidae)
Quick ID: small, olive-green, broken white eye ring; male—red crown patch; female—green crown
Length: 4.25" Weight: 0.23 oz. Wingspan: 7.5"

You may hear the high-pitched staccato "zee-zee-zee" scolding of king-lets before you see these tiny birds as they announce their alarm call. However, weighing only about as much as a quarter, you have little to fear from these petite birds. Both ruby-crowned kinglets and golden-crowned kinglets can be seen along the Parkway. When agitated, males of both kinglet species raise hidden crown patches, red on the ruby-crown and yellow-orange on the golden-crown. To identify them look for the white eye ring on the ruby-crowns while golden-crowns have a white eye line with a black crown. Look for kinglets on the Tanawha Trail, Craggy Gardens, and Mount Mitchell State Park.

RED-BREASTED NUTHATCH
Sitta canadensis
Nuthatch family (Sittidae)
Quick ID: bluish-gray back, pale-orange belly, black line through eyes topped by a white line, white chin, black cap
Length: 4.5"   Weight: 0.35 oz.   Wingspan: 8.5"

In the South the red-breasted nuthatch breeds in the Blue Ridge in high-altitude spruce-fir and coniferous forests. They are easily recognized by their nasal toy-horn calls of "yank-yank-yank." The larger white-breasted nuthatch is the more common nuthatch of lower elevations. Nuthatches break open nuts by wedging them into cracks in tree bark and hacking at them until the seed pops out. Look for red-breasted nuthatches at Craggy Gardens, Linville Falls, Mount Pisgah, and Heintooga Spur Road. They are also a common visitor to bird feeders at the privately owned Grandfather Mountain just off the Parkway. Nuthatches often climb headfirst down trees searching for insects, while brown creepers with mottled brown feathers and long, spiky tails spiral up trees.

BARRED OWL
Strix varia
Owl family (Strigidae)
Quick ID: large, gray-brown back with white markings, lacks ear tufts, pale-gray facial disc, black eyes, horizontal bars on head and neck, vertical brown streaks on yellowish-white belly
Length: 21" Weight: 1.6 lbs. Wingspan: 42"

As the curtain of dusk gently falls, the nightly chorus of the southern Appalachians tunes up with the melodic cacophony of katydids, spring peepers, and locusts. One of the most recognizable of all calls is the sentence-like call of the barred owl questioning, "who cooks for you, who cooks for you all," with the last syllable descending and drawn out. A large owl with a rounded head and dark eyes, the barred owl lacks the ear tufts of the larger great horned owl. Unlike most nocturnal owls, the barred owl can sometimes be active during the day and may be seen perched on a tree limb listening for the scamper of prey in the underbrush.

SCARLET TANAGER
Piranga olivacea
Tanager family (Thraupidae)
Quick ID: male—brilliant red, black wings, black tail; female—greenish yellow, olive-brown wings
Length: 7" Weight: 0.98 oz. Wingspan: 11.5"

Scarlet tanagers top the list of many birders who enjoy watching these gorgeous birds. The striking male sports plumage with a scarlet-red base offset by black wings and a black tail. The less showy female is dull greenish yellow, which aids in camouflage while nesting. The other tanager that can be spotted at low elevations along the Parkway is the summer tanager. The male is rose red overall without the black wings and tail of the scarlet tanager. The female summer tanager is similar to the female scarlet tanager but has less contrast between the wings and back. Look for scarlet tanagers at Mabry Mill, Altapass, and Heintooga Spur Road.

RUBY-THROATED HUMMINGBIRD
Archilochus colubris
Hummingbird family (Trochilidae)
Quick ID: iridescent-green back and crown; long, thin bill; male—ruby-red throat; female—white throat
Length: 3.75" Weight: 0.11 oz. Wingspan: 4.5"

The only hummingbird regularly found in the East, the ruby-throated hummingbird is easy to distinguish from all other birds. At first glance hummingbirds may look like large insects or bees, but they are tiny birds with some amazing characteristics. Unique in the world of birds, "hummers" possess the ability to fly backward and hover in midair. Hummingbirds can beat their wings up to 75 times per second and zip in and away from their flower-nectar source with rapid precision. The female has a white throat, and the ruby-red throat of the male can look blackish when it is not in good light. Look for these delightful birds nectaring at orange or red tubular flowers including cardinal flower, wild columbine, spotted jewelweed, and bee balm.

AMERICAN ROBIN
Turdus migratorius
Thrush family (Turdidae)
Quick ID: upperparts gray to black, breast and underparts reddish orange
Length: 10" Weight: 2.7 oz. Wingspan: 17"

One of the most familiar of all birds, the American robin is native to North America but is named for a European robin that is similar in coloration but unrelated. In spring robins build a cup-shaped nest of twigs, grass, and mud in which they lay from 3 to 5 sky-blue eggs. After hatching, the young are ready to fledge in only about 2 weeks. They remain undercover in bushes or trees, often fluttering their wings and begging for food from their parents, who continue to care for the chicks. In an effort to protect their offspring, the parents will often dive-bomb predators. The brown spotted chicks develop rapidly and are soon able to feed themselves.

EASTERN BLUEBIRD
Sialia sialis
Thrush family (Turdidae)
Quick ID: orangish chest and sides, white belly; male—bright-blue head and upperparts; female—dull blue
Length: 7" Weight: 1.1 oz. Wingspan: 13"

The passionate subjects of songs, poems, and love stories, bluebirds are a welcome sight in spring and according to folklore a sign of sure happiness. The poster bird of conservation efforts, bluebird populations experienced a sharp decline in numbers in the 1960s due to habitat destruction. Proactive nature lovers began setting up and monitoring bluebird boxes. Their efforts have reversed the downward trend, and now bluebirds are a common sight in the East. Look for them sitting on fences and wires in open areas along the Parkway. Other eastern birds that are blue include blue jays, which are much larger; male indigo buntings, which are entirely blue; and cerulean and black-throated blue warblers, which are smaller than the other blue birds.

EASTERN PHOEBE
Sayornis phoebe
Tyrant flycatcher family (Tyrannidae)
Quick ID: grayish brown above, pale creamy yellowish below, lacks eye ring, dark bill
Length: 7" Weight: 0.7 oz. Wingspan: 10.5"

"Wag your tail feathers" may be the best descriptive characteristic of this rather plain-colored bird in the flycatcher family. One of the earliest birds to arrive back to North Carolina and Virginia in the spring, they announce their arrival with a raspy "fee-bee" song from which they get their name. The tail-bobbing practice is a distinctive feature to look for as the bird sits on branches watching for a passing insect. Eastern wood pewees, flycatchers, and the eastern kingbird are members of the tyrant flycatcher family, and they all feed on insects that they catch in flight in a practice called "hawking." Phoebes often build their nests under the eaves of buildings or bridges.

RED-EYED VIREO
Vireo olivaceus
Vireo family (Vireonidae)
Quick ID: olive-green upperparts, white underparts, gray crown, white eyebrow, gray line through eye, red iris
Length: 6" Weight: 0.6 oz. Wingspan: 10"

The red-eyed vireo is a small songbird commonly found along the Parkway. Resembling large warblers, vireos have a hook on the end of their thick bill. Quite an outgoing bird, the red-eyed vireo whistles a song that sounds like "look-up-way-up-in-the-trees." Researchers have counted male red-eyed vireos singing more than 10,000 songs a day in the spring. Vireos eat a wide variety of insects including beetles, mosquitoes, wasps, and ants. In addition to the red-eyed vireo, 3 other vireo species can be found in the Blue Ridge: blue-headed, warbling, and yellow-throated. Look for red-eyed vireos along Heintooga Spur Road, Altapass, and Humpback Rocks.

EASTERN AMERICAN TOAD
Anaxyrus americanus
Toad family (Bufonidae)
Quick ID: large; dark spots, each with a wart; variable color from gray to brown to reddish
Length: 2"–3.5"

In March and April eastern American toads congregate in shallow breeding pools to lay their eggs, which hatch into tadpoles in about a week or two. The tadpoles stay in their watery pool for about 2 months, during which time they undergo metamorphosis, grow legs, and begin to breathe above water. Mostly nocturnal, the adults hide under logs and leaves during the day.

COPE'S GRAY TREEFROG
Hyla chrysoscelis
Treefrog family (Hylidae)
Quick ID: grayish or green, large dark blotches on back, concealed bright orange on hind legs
Length: 1.25"–2"

Cope's gray treefrog is found along the Parkway mainly in North Carolina, while its identical look-alike, the gray treefrog (*H. versicolor*), is found along the Virginia portion of the Parkway. The only way to tell the 2 apart is by their trilling call, with the sound of the Cope's treefrog shorter, harsher, and more forceful than that of the gray treefrog.

SPRING PEEPER
Pseudacris crucifer
Tree frog family (Hylidae)
Quick ID: tan, brown, or gray, dark lines that form an X on back, pointed snout
Length: 0.75"–1.5"

The high, clear peeping notes of the call of the spring peeper signal the end of winter and the return of spring. Rarely seen, these nocturnal choristers tune up at dusk, and a group of males calling for mates may be so loud that they can be heard over a mile away.

BLUE RIDGE DUSKY SALAMANDER
Desmognathus orestes
Lungless salamander family (Plethodontidae)
Quick ID: medium-size; eyeline from eye to mouth; rounded tail; variable yellow, brown, orange, or reddish dorsal stripe pattern
Length: 3"–4.5"

The Blue Ridge dusky salamander was once placed in the same species as 3 other salamanders, but recent genetic testing has distinguished these into 4 separate species including Carolina mountain dusky (*D. carolinensis*), Allegheny mountain dusky (*D. ochrophaeus*), and Ocoee salamander (*D. ocoee*). All abundant with their ranges, the number of Carolina mountain duskies reaches more than 2,500 individuals per acre in some areas. They all look very similar in appearance and are best separated by location. The Blue Ridge dusky salamander is the northernmost of the group and is found in southern Virginia and northern North Carolina along the Parkway. Blue Ridge dusky salamanders can be found in seepage areas, wet rock faces, and near streams and seeps.

BLUE RIDGE TWO-LINED SALAMANDER
Eurycea wilderae
Lungless salamander family (Plethodontidae)
Quick ID: small, slender, yellow-orange back with 2 black stripes that break up into spots midway down the tail, sides with black irregular spots
Length: 2.75"–4.75"

The Blue Ridge two-lined salamander can be found at high elevations along the Parkway in North Carolina and southern Virginia. They are brightly colored salamanders that often remain in or near streams. Lungless salamanders absorb oxygen through their moist skin.

EASTERN RED-BACKED SALAMANDER
Plethodon cinereus
Lungless salamander family (Plethodontidae)
Quick ID: either striped red back or unstriped lead-backed lacking the dorsal stripe
Length: 2.25"–5"

Even though salamanders are not commonly seen, in some areas their numbers can exceed all other vertebrates. One of the most common salamanders in their range, eastern red-backed salamanders will defend their territories against other salamanders. They produce noxious skin secretions to deter predators.

NORTHERN GRAY-CHEEKED SALAMANDER
Plethodon montanus
Lungless salamander family (Plethodontidae)
Quick ID: dark-gray body, light-gray cheeks
Length: 3.5"–5"

A southern Appalachian specialty, gray-cheeked salamanders are found at relatively higher elevation areas along the Parkway. In their woodland habitats they hunt for insects and small invertebrates at night under cover of darkness. During the day they shelter under rocks or logs.

PEAKS OF OTTER SALAMANDER
Plethodon hubrichti
Lungless salamander family (Plethodontidae)
Quick ID: black with brassy specks on back, few white spots on cheeks and sides
Length: 3"–5"

In 3 counties in Virginia lives a distinctive salamander called the Peaks of Otter salamander. Found nowhere else in the world, this population of small speckled salamanders is endemic to an area near Peaks of Otter on the Parkway. This salamander has one of the most restricted ranges in the United States, and the Blue Ridge Parkway helps to protect its vital habitat. Peaks of Otter salamanders never stray far from their home territory, which may be under a rock or log. They venture out at night, especially after a rain, to feed on ants, springtails, and other small invertebrates. This small population of salamanders remains to tell the story of a long-forgotten and now extinct ancestral salamander.

YONAHLOSSEE SALAMANDER
Plethodon yonahlossee
Lungless salamander family (Plethodontidae)
Quick ID: black back with brick-red blotches or solid wide band, sides with heavy grayish-white blotches or band
Length: 4.5"–7.5"

A large and distinctively marked salamander, the Yonahlossee salamander has reddish-brown blotches that often fuse into a wide band as it ages. *Yonahlossee* is a Native American word that means "trail of the bear," indicating the Yonahlossee Road just northeast of Linville, North Carolina, where the species was first described in 1917.

EASTERN SNAPPING TURTLE
Chelydra serpentina
Snapping turtle family (Chelydridae)
Quick ID: brownish overall, flattened upper shell (carapace) with ridges, long saw-toothed tail, large head with blunt protruding snout and hooked jaw
Length: shell 8"–19"

Snapping turtles date back 65 million years, and these primitive-looking but powerful creatures live in the ponds, streams, and lakes of the Blue Ridge Parkway. Snappers often bury themselves in the mud with only their nostrils and eyes exposed, waiting for a passing meal of fish, frogs, crayfish, insects, or even ducks or muskrats. These turtles have powerful hooked jaws that they employ with lightning fast speed. They have long, flexible necks and can easily reach beside their shell. The average weight is between 10 and 35 pounds, but the record holder weighed in at 75 pounds. Snappers provided early settlers with the main ingredient for turtle soup, and their shells were used as containers.

NORTHERN WATER SNAKE
Nerodia sipedon
Colubrid family (Colubridae)
Quick ID: dark brown with square dark blotches, aquatic
Length: 24"–42"

Usually found in or near water, the northern water snake is often a victim of mistaken identity. Because of its affinity for water, it is often confused with the poisonous cottonmouth or "water moccasin," which does not occur on the Parkway. Water snakes are found in ponds, streams, rivers, and wetlands along the Parkway. They prey on fish, frogs, crayfish, and small mammals found in or along the edges of waterways. These water snakes are prey for many predators including raccoons, snapping turtles, foxes, and other snakes. They defend themselves vigorously when threatened and will bite repeatedly. Their saliva contains an anticoagulant which causes profuse bleeding, but they are not poisonous.

ROUGH GREEN SNAKE
Opheodrys aestivus
Colubrid family (Colubridae)
Quick ID: thin, bright green above, yellowish belly, keeled dorsal scales
Length: 22"–37"

A green beauty, the rough green snake is an agile climber but is difficult to see as it blends well with foliage of trees and shrubs. During the day they forage for insects along the edges of streams and ponds, helping to keep the insect populations in check. They spend nights coiled in tree branches. Fairly docile, rough green snakes are nonvenomous and seldom bite when handled. They have many predators including larger snakes and hawks, and their best defense is camouflage.

EASTERN BOX TURTLE
Terrapene carolina
Box and pond turtle family (Emydidae)
Quick ID: highly domed brown top shell (carapace) with variable yellow markings, head and neck brown with orange to yellow markings, hinged underside (plastron)
Length: shell 4.5"–8.5"

The eastern box turtle holds the honor of representing the reptile world as the state reptile of North Carolina. Box turtles are medium-size turtles that are highly variable in shell coloration and patterns. The shell is highly domed and smooth on the rear edge. Box turtles can live to be over 50 years old and don't reach full adulthood until they are 7 to 10 years old. Box turtles are terrestrial and are found in wooded areas and field edges. Omnivores, they eat berries, snails, beetles, caterpillars, mushrooms, and even salamanders. In winter they bury themselves beneath leaf piles, logs, or grass clumps. Seven turtle species can be found along the Parkway including the endangered bog turtle, *Clemmys muhlenbergii*.

EASTERN FENCE LIZARD
Sceloporus undulatus
Spiny lizard family (Phrynosomatidae)
Quick ID: grayish-brown cross-band patterned, rough-keeled pointed overlapping scales
Length: 4"–7"

The aptly named eastern fence lizard is often seen stretched out on a fence post or log soaking up the morning sun. If approached, they scamper to the nearest tree, where they swiftly climb up the trunk. If you approach closer, they shimmy to the opposite side of the tree and will play this game until they eventually climb high up into the branches and out of reach. To advertise their territory to other fence lizards, males flash their bright-blue chin and side patches. Eastern 5-lined skinks (*Plestiodon fasciatus*) and broad-headed skinks (*P. laticeps*) are 2 of the other handful of lizards that can be found along the Parkway.

NORTHERN COPPERHEAD
Agkistrodon contortrix
Pit viper family (Viperidae)
Quick ID: coppery-red triangular head, hourglass pattern, vertical pupils
Length: 24"–36"

Also called chunkheads, copperheads have a thick triangular head, elliptical pupils like a cat, and a distinctive hourglass pattern along their backs. When approached by humans, copperheads will often freeze in an attempt to camouflage themselves against the forest floor or rock ledge where they are often found. Bites to humans are almost never fatal but can be quite painful. Always watch where you put your hands or feet especially when climbing over rocks or logs. If bitten, seek medical attention as soon as possible. Scientists are researching the medicinal use of copperhead venom as an anticancer drug that has been shown to be an effective combatant in halting the growth of new blood vessels to cancerous tumors.

TIMBER RATTLESNAKE
Crotalus horridus
Pit viper family (Viperidae)
Quick ID: triangular head, elliptical pupils, yellow phase with dark cross bands, black phase with black head and black marks on dark-grayish-brown body
Length: 36"–60"

About 15 species of snakes can be found along the Parkway, but only 2 of them are poisonous: the timber rattlesnake and the northern copperhead. Timber rattlesnakes are especially fond of sunny, rocky outcroppings and ledges. Make sure to watch where you put your hands and feet when walking or climbing on rocky places. They will often give a warning rattle if threatened. The rattle is composed of hollow segments made of keratin, just like your fingernails. A new rattle segment is added every time a snake sheds its skin, which may be 2 to 4 times per year. Rattlesnakes rarely bite unless threatened or provoked, and bites are rarely fatal if treated promptly with antivenom.

BLUEGILL
Lepomis macrochirus
Sunfish family (Centrarchidae)
Quick ID: laterally flattened olive-brown body, 6–8 dark vertical bars on sides, belly yellowish orange, dark smudge on posterior base of dorsal fin, ear flap short and dark, iridescent-blue cheek and gill cover
Length: 4"–12" Weight: 1–8 oz.

The bluegill, which is commonly called brim or bream, is a popular pan-fish, so called because it can fit nicely into a frying pan. A favorite with anglers, bluegills can be found in ponds, lakes, and quiet streams, often hiding under shaded shorelines, downed trees, or along weed beds. The similar pumpkinseed (*L. gibbosus*) has a reddish spot on a black ear flap.

REDBREAST SUNFISH
Lepomis auritus
Sunfish family (Centrarchidae)
Quick ID: long, narrow black earflap; wavy blue lines on cheek; olive back; rows of orangish spots on sides; breeding male has orange underparts, red in fins
Length: 4"–12" Weight: 0.25–1.7 lbs.

Members of the sunfish family are sometimes called bream, but the term actually refers to a type of European freshwater fish. With an average length of 6 to 8 inches, redbreast sunfish have wavy blue lines on their cheeks and rows of orangish spots on their sides. The black earflap is the longest of any sunfish and may reach 1 inch in length. The bluegill, another sunfish, has a black dot on the dorsal fin. Look for redbreast sunfish in the Otter Creek aquatic system, especially around overhanging banks and in the cool shadows of trees and shrubs.

SMALLMOUTH BASS
Micropterus dolomieu
Sunfish family (Centrarchidae)
Quick ID: bronzy brownish green, 3 dark bars behind eye, vertical bars on sides, red eyes
Length: 10"–24" Weight: 1–8.6 lbs.

Names can be relative, and the smallmouth bass was dubbed smallmouth because its relative the largemouth bass has a bigger mouth. Unlike the mouth of the largemouth bass, the upper jaw does not extend beyond the eye in the smallmouth. The smallmouth has vertical bars on the sides, compared with the horizontal band on the largemouth. Found in clear mountain streams and foothill ponds, lakes, and rivers, the smallmouth bass is one of the most exciting fish to challenge the rods of anglers. With a state fishing permit, visitors to the Blue Ridge Parkway can try their hand at this feisty catch. Make sure to check the fishing regulations on the official Parkway website (www.nps.gov/blri/parkmgmt/lawsandpolicies.htm).

BLUE RIDGE SCULPIN
Cottus caeruleomentum
Sculpin family (Cottidae)
Quick ID: light-brown flattened body, dark mottling on sides, eyes high on head, dorsal fins joined at base
Length: 3"–4" Weight: 0.47–0.65 oz.

Recent genetic research has shown that the Blue Ridge sculpin, which is found in streams in the northern section of the Blue Ridge Parkway, is not the same species that it was once thought to be. Nearly identical to the closely related mottled sculpin (*C. bairdii*), it blends easily into the gravelly riffles of streams. Sculpins are so highly camouflaged that 2 US Navy submarines were named to honor this small fish.

WARPAINT SHINER
Luxilus coccogenis
Carp and minnow family (Cyprinidae)
Quick ID: silver body, olive-gray on top, dark band on dorsal and tail fins, orange line on cheek, orange-red fins in breeding males
Length: 3.5"–5.5" Weight: 0.2 oz.

An Appalachian endemic, the warpaint shiner lives up to its name, boasting streaks of red and black as if they were deliberately painted on to intimidate other minnows. Often overlooked, minnows play an important role in the ecosystem as they keep the small insect population in check and provide food for larger fish.

EASTERN BROOK TROUT
Salvelinus fontinalis
Trout family (Salmonidae)
Quick ID: dark-olive-green to brown, cream wavy lines (vermiculations) on back and head, sides with pale spots and red spots with bluish halos, bottom fins white-edged
Length: 5"–9.8"   Weight: 2.2–13.2 lbs.

Brook trout are the only native trout in the East. The other 2 trout found in Parkway waters are introduced: the rainbow trout (*Oncorhynchus mykiss*) from the western United States and the brown trout (*Salmo trutta*) from Europe. Brook trout thrive in clean, cold streams with temperatures below 68°F. Pulling in a "brookie" is a delight for anglers, but catch-and-release practices are preferred to allow these natives to survive in the wild. Fishing is allowed on Parkway waters with a valid North Carolina or Virginia fishing license. Only single-hook, artificial lures may be used. Some streams and lakes have specific posted regulations. Please see the official Blue Ridge Parkway website (www.nps.gov/blri/parkmgmt/lawsandpolicies.htm) for more information on fishing regulations.

RAINBOW TROUT
Oncorhynchus mykiss
Trout family (Salmonidae)
Quick ID: olive-green, small blackish spots on sides and fins, pinkish stripe on sides and cheeks
Length: 10"–16" Weight: 2–6 lbs.

Named for the colorful pinkish stripe on its sides, the rainbow trout is originally native to the western United States and was introduced in the 1800s into eastern waters as a popular game fish. Along with the brown trout (*Salmo trutta*), which was introduced from Europe, the rainbow trout is a voracious feeder, often outcompeting the native brook trout (*Salvelinus fontinalis*) where they are found together. The brown trout has black spots and red spots with blue halos and an unspotted tail. The rainbow trout fares best in streams with cool, fast-moving waters. Brown trout prefer larger, slower-flowing streams with ample minnows for food. Valid North Carolina or Virginia fishing licenses are required for anglers. Check the Parkway website (www.nps.gov/blri/parkmgmt/lawsandpolicies.htm) for complete fishing regulations.

SILVER-SPOTTED SKIPPER
Epargyreus clarus
Skipper family (Hesperiidae)
Quick ID: brown, lobed hindwing, gold spots on forewing, silvery-white blotch on underside of hindwing
Wingspan: 1.75"–2.63"
Flight season: March–October

Typically, skippers are small, brown butterflies that usually go unnoticed, but the relatively large silver-spotted skipper is so widespread that many Parkway visitors are curious about this common butterfly. This skipper seems to shun yellow flowers, preferring pink, purple, red, and blue flowers.

SUMMER AZURE
Celastrina neglecta
Gossamer-wing family (Lycaenidae)
Quick ID: small, powdery blue, chalky white below with faint dark spots
Wingspan: 0.75"–1.13"
Flight season: April–September

Small blue butterflies may be seen daintily nectaring from flowers, but they may be difficult to identify. Spring azures (*C. laden*) fly in spring but are then replaced by the summer azures. The eastern-tailed blue (*Everes comyntas*) has threadlike tails, and the males are vibrant blue with 2 orange hindwing spots, while the females are dusky bluish brown.

COMMON BUCKEYE
Junonia coenia
Brushfoot family
(Nymphalidae)
Quick ID: brown, large eyespots, orange bands on forewing
Wingspan: 1.63"–2.75"
Flight season: March–November

A very abundant butterfly, the common buckeye is named for the large eyespots on its wings. The multicolored spots, which resemble large eyes, are a form of protection intended to frighten away would-be predators such as birds. They fly low to the ground, nectaring on asters, sunflowers, and dogbane.

GREAT SPANGLED FRITILLARY
Speyeria cybele
Brushfoot family (Nymphalidae)
Quick ID: large, orange with black markings, silver spots on underwings
Wingspan: 2.5"–4"
Flight season: May–October

Great spangled fritillaries are large orange butterflies often seen in summer soaring over fields and flower-filled meadows. The variegated fritillary (*Euptoieta claudia*) is smaller and lacks the silver markings on the underwings. Another orange butterfly, the pearl crescent (*Phyciodes tharos*) is smaller yet with black wing borders.

MONARCH
Danaus plexippus
Brushfoot family (Nymphalidae)
Quick ID: orange with black veins, white spots
on black wing borders
Wingspan: 3.38"–4.88"
Flight season: April–November

Each year in late September, thousands of monarch butterflies glide silently over the rolling blue mountains of the Parkway. Floating on paper-thin orange wings, the monarchs begin their journey southward to spend the winter in Mexico. Joining the procession of monarchs are migrating dragonflies, whose thin bodies catch the sun's rays and reflect the dazzling greens and blues as they dart erratically through the crisp fall air. During the last 2 weeks of September, find an open space, spread a blanket, and enjoy a picnic lunch while you watch for the silent overhead parade. Some favorite areas to enjoy the migration are Harvey's Knob (MP 94.5), Doughton Park (MP 240), Alta Pass (MP 328), and Wagon Road Gap (MP 412.2).

QUESTION MARK
Polygonia interrogationis
Brushfoot family (Nymphalidae)
Quick ID: reddish orange, angled wings, silver
comma with dot on underside of hindwing
Wingspan: 2.38"–3"
Flight season: March–November

"Question mark" seems like a funny name for a butterfly, but if you look closely at the underside of the hindwing, you will notice a small silver comma with a dot that resembles a question mark, leading to a perfectly good explanation for the common name. The summer form of the question mark has a mostly black hindwing, while the fall form is lighter and has a violet edging to the wings. Camouflaged from predators, the folded wings look like dead leaves.

RED-SPOTTED PURPLE
Limenitis arthemis
Brushfoot family (Nymphalidae)
Quick ID: black with iridescent blue on upper-wings, row of red-orange spots underwing
Wingspan: 2.5"–2.75"
Flight season: April–October

The iridescent-blue coloration on black wings often reflects the sunlight as this butterfly puddles (sips nutrients and minerals) in the mud or on rotting fruit. As it flies away you will notice a band of red-orange spots on the underwings. Very similar in coloration to the toxic pipevine swallowtail (*Battus philenor*), would-be predators avoid this butterfly once they have gotten a taste of the "pipevine."

EASTERN TIGER SWALLOWTAIL
Papilio glaucus
Swallowtail family (Papilionidae)
Quick ID: large yellow or black, vertical black stripes, blue and orange markings on hindwings
Wingspan: 2.5"–4.5"
Flight season: March–October

The large, yellow, tiger-striped wings of the eastern tiger swallowtail are easily identifiable markings for this common butterfly. At least it is easy until you learn that the female may also be black rather than yellow. The coloration of the black females provides them some protection from predators as they mimic pipevine swallowtails (*Battus philenor*), which are distastefully toxic to potential predators. The pipevine swallowtail has iridescent-blue coloration on the hindwings. The dark female lacks the band of orange spots on the hindwing of the spicebush and black swallowtails. The official state butterfly of Virginia, this swallowtail nectars on many flowers including milkweed, bee balm, lilies, phlox, and joe-pye weed. Food plants for the caterpillars include black cherry and tulip tree.

PIPEVINE SWALLOWTAIL
Battus philenor
Swallowtail family (Papilionidae)
Quick ID: dark forewing, iridescent-blue or blue-green hindwing, white spots, band of orange spots underneath
Wingspan: 2.5"–4.25"
Flight season: April–September

One of the large dark butterflies that you may see along the Parkway is the pipevine swallowtail. Notice the iridescent-blue or blue-green coloration on the upper hindwings, which lack the orange spots of the other large dark butterflies such as spicebush and black swallowtails. The larvae feed on various pipevine species including Dutchman's pipe and Virginia snakeroot. In spring the adults lay their eggs on the large shady leaves of Dutchman's pipe. The spiny, black, red-dotted caterpillars that emerge later munch on the toxic leaves and retain that toxicity as adults, which aids in protection against predators. Adult pipevine swallowtails feed at a wide variety of flowers including lilies, milkweeds, thistles, and bergamot.

SPICEBUSH SWALLOWTAIL
Papilio troilus
Swallowtail family (Papilionidae)
Quick ID: black with white marginal spots, upper hindwing dusty blue, underside hindwing with 2 rows of orange spots
Wingspan: 2.5"–4.5"
Flight season: April–September

Butterflies provide an amazing view into their life cycle. They lay their eggs on specific plants, and when the young hatch out, they are in the form of a caterpillar. This caterpillar, or larva, chows down on the plant leaf where it had been attached as an egg. The caterpillars molt or shed their skin 4 or more times as they grow. The last skin shedding reveals the pupa, or chrysalis, and many species overwinter in this stage. While in the chrysalis, the caterpillar tissues break down and are transformed into the adult insect structures that emerge in spring as adult butterflies. The spicebush swallowtail is named for one of the caterpillar food plants called spicebush (*Lindera benzoin*).

ZEBRA SWALLOWTAIL
Eurytides marcellus
Swallowtail family
(Papilionidae)
Quick ID: white with black stripes, long
slender tails, upper hindwings with red
patch, red stripe on underwings
Wingspan: 2.5"–4"
Flight season: April–October

The appropriately named zebra swallowtail sports black zebra stripes on dull white wings. They fly rapidly and low amid the understory, trailing long, thin tails behind them. Look for these beautiful butterflies flitting about their larval food plant the pawpaw (*Asimina triloba*) near the James River Visitor Center.

CABBAGE WHITE
Pieris rapae
White and sulphur family
(Pieridae)
Quick ID: white to yellowish white,
forewing with black tip, females have
1 black spot on the wings, males have
2 black spots
Wingspan: 1.25"–1.75"
Flight season: March–November

The sight of a small green caterpillar with thin yellow racing stripes gnawing away on neat rows of cabbage, broccoli, or radishes sent gardeners to pluck them off and drop them into old coffee cans with a bit of kerosene in the bottom. Today insecticides are used. Introduced in the 1800s, the caterpillars of the cabbage white butterfly cause significant crop damage and are considered a detrimental pest.

ORANGE SULPHUR
Colias eurytheme
White and sulphur family
(Pieridae)
Quick ID: underside yellow, upper
side orange with black margin
Wingspan: 1.5"–2.4"
Flight Season: March–October

One of the most abundant
butterflies in the fields and meadows along the Parkway is the orange sulphur. The colors are variable, but orange on the upper wings with a black
margin and yellow underside characterize this butterfly. The clouded
sulphur, *C. philodice,* is similar but has no orange on the wings. The
caterpillars feed on alfalfa and clovers. Adults nectar from many flowers including asters, milkweeds, and goldenrods. The adults may be seen
sipping moisture from wet soil and mud puddles in a behavior known as
"puddling." The butterflies obtain salts and other nutrients from the soil.
They may also sip nutrients from urine, dung, and carrion.

HUMMINGBIRD CLEARWING MOTH
Hemaris thysbe
Sphinx moth family
(Sphingidae)
Quick ID: golden-olive back, yellow
belly, dark-burgundy abdomen, wings
mostly clear with dark reddish borders
Wingspan: 1.5"–2.25"
Flight season: March–October

Most moths are active only at night, but some, like the hummingbird
clearwing moth, fly during the day. Often mistaken for small hummingbirds, these moths hover at flowers to sip nectar with a long coiled
needlelike mouthpart called a proboscis that the moth uncoils to dip into
a flower. They may be seen at tubular flowers such as phlox, bee balm,
thistles, and honeysuckles.

GREEN DARNER

Anax junius
Darner family (Aeshnidae)
Quick ID: male—green with blue abdomen and black markings; female—green with reddish abdomen
Length: 2.7"–3.1"

Fierce predators that defend their watery territories, dragonflies live up to their name and are often seen swooping down upon smaller insects at great speeds. Other imaginative common names include snake doctor, darning needle, and mosquito hawk. Dragonflies cannot sting and only deliver a tiny bite if threatened while they are being handled. The green darner is one of the largest dragonflies with a wingspan reaching up to 4 inches. Some green darners migrate south for the winter, and it is their offspring that make the return trip back. In the fall large numbers often follow ridgelines along the Parkway as they join with migrating birds and monarchs to make the long journey south for the winter.

HONEYBEE
Apis mellifera
Honeybee family (Apidae)
Quick ID: reddish brown with hairs, abdomen black with yellowish-orange bands
Length: 0.5"–0.63"

For many settlers to the Blue Ridge, honey was one of their only sources of sweetener, and beehives were often kept for a ready supply. Even today, beekeepers place their hives near sourwood trees for the unique taste that the blooms give to the honey. Prized by local residents, sourwood honey is often sold at roadside stands. Early European settlers introduced honeybees to North America in the 1600s. Resourceful homemakers modified their recipes for use of honey as a sweetener rather than granulated sugar, which was difficult to obtain. Honey was added to soap to moisturize skin and was used to heal wounds. A wick made of spun cotton was added to beeswax to make candles.

GOLDEN GARDEN SPIDER
Argiope aurantia
Orb weaver family (Araneidae)
Quick ID: black with bright yellow markings
Length: female 0.75"–1.13", male 0.25"–0.38"

Perhaps the female doesn't realize that she advertises bright yellow warning colors, but she does know that she is big and the queen of her domain. The female golden garden spider, or Argiope (pronounced ar-GUY-oh-pee), is much larger than the male. The circular web she spins can be over 2 feet in diameter, and her zigzag weaving adorns the center. Insect prey, such as flies, mosquitoes, wasps, and bees, that are trapped in the sticky web are paralyzed with venom, wrapped securely, and saved for a future meal. These spiders will only bite humans if provoked, and the bite is harmless. Only 2 spiders in our area—the black widow and the brown recluse—are potentially dangerous.

WOOLLY BEAR CATERPILLAR
Pyrrharctia isabella
Tiger moth family (Arctiidae)
Quick ID: coppery-red in middle, black at both ends
Length: 2"–3"

Pioneers knew that the colorful leaves of fall meant that the cold winds of winter would soon be upon them. They used many methods to try to predict the severity of the upcoming winter, including the relative thickness of hulls on hickory nuts and the activity of squirrels gathering the nuts. Perhaps the best-known folktale predictor was the amount of brown fuzzed segments on the woolly bear caterpillar, or "woolly worm" as it is locally called. In October you can celebrate the illustrious caterpillar at the Woolly Worm Festival just off the Parkway at MP 304 in Banner Elk, North Carolina. In spring the adult emerges as a dull orangish-yellow moth called the Isabella tiger moth.

EBONY JEWELWING
Calopteryx maculata
Broad-winged damselfly family (Calopterygidae)
Quick ID: metallic-green damselfly with black wings
Length: 1.5"–2"

These black-winged ebony jewelwing damselflies are brilliantly colored metallic and may shimmer blue in the sunlight. Damselflies can be seen around ponds and streams, often sitting on a twig or blade of grass with their wings folded up. Dragonflies typically hold their wings in a horizontal position when resting. Female ebony jewelwings have a speck of white on their wingtips.

MILKWEED BEETLE
Tetraopes tetrophthalmus
Long-horned beetle family
(Cerambycidae)
Quick ID: bright orange-red with black
spots, legs blackish, long blackish antenna
Length: 0.38"–0.5"

To say that beetles are everywhere may be an understatement, as 1 in every 5 species of living organisms (including plants) on earth is a beetle. One out of every 4 animals is a beetle. Many beetles, such as the milkweed beetle, advertise their toxicity with bright red, orange, or yellow warning colors. The milkweed beetle feeds on milkweeds, absorbing the plant's toxic latex. With the same tactics as the monarch butterfly, the beetle becomes distasteful to would-be predators that learn to avoid the bright-red beetle. The larvae overwinter in the milkweed roots, and adults emerge in June. The adults can make squeaking sounds by rubbing areas on their thorax.

PERIODICAL CICADA
Magicicada spp.
Cicada family (Cicadidae)
Quick ID: bulging red eyes, black body,
orange underneath, wings clear with
orange veins
Length: 0.9"–1.3"

Living underground into their teens, periodical cicadas have one of the most fascinating life cycles of all creatures. Sometimes called "17-year locusts," these insects surface every 13 or 17 years in May and June, shed their exoskeletons, and emerge as winged adults. With a characteristic buzzy drone, males begin noisily attracting females. After mating, the females lay their eggs in end twigs of deciduous trees, causing the tips to turn brown and flag downward. After hatching, the nymphs drop to the ground, burrow about a foot underground, and live off the sugars of tree roots. Emerging annually in late July and August, the mottled green annual or "dog-day" cicadas in the genus *Tibicen* lack the red eyes.

ACORN WEEVIL
Curculio spp.
Weevil family (Curculionidae)
Quick ID: long, thin decurved snout; robust brown body
Length: 0.38"

Equipped with a miniature saw, acorn weevils use their long snouts to carve holes into acorns by circling round and round until the shells are punctured. The females lay their eggs inside the acorn, where the larvae mature. When fully grown the larvae chew a round 0.13-inch hole in the shell, exit, and enter the soil, where they remain for 1 to 2 years before emerging as adults.

NORTHERN WALKINGSTICK
Diapheromera femorata
Stick insect family (Diapheromeridae)
Quick ID: brown, long, thin body
Length: body 3"–3.75"

The dachshund of the insect world, walking sticks have extremely thin, cylindrical bodies. Their antennae are about ⅔ the length of their 3-inch body. Birds are their most common predator, and when threatened walkingsticks can remain motionless and are amazingly camouflaged as twigs. They consume the leaves of trees, especially favoring oaks and hazelnuts.

GRAY-FOOTED LANCETOOTH SNAIL
Haplotrema concavum
Predatory land snail family (Haplotrematidae)
Quick ID: land snail, shiny whorled shell greenish white to light yellow, opening rounded
Length: 0.4"–0.8"

While most snails go meekly about eating fungi and decaying leaves and wood called detritus, there is a group of predatory snails that attack other snails. The gray-footed lancetooth is one such snail that uses its rough tongue, called a radula, to file apart the shell of its victim. Slugs are similar to snails, but they are not born with a protective external shell like the one snails have.

AMERICAN DOG TICK
Dermacentor variabilis
Hard tick family (Ixodidae)
Quick ID: flat, reddish brown with silvery-gray markings, 8 legs as adult, 4 legs as nymph
Length: 0.14"–0.19"

For a creature about the size of a sunflower seed kernel, the American dog tick can cause a lot of trouble. This tick and its relative the brown dog tick (*Rhipicephalus sanguineus*) can carry bacteria that cause Rocky Mountain spotted fever, which can be fatal. North Carolina has one of the highest incidence rates of Rocky Mountain spotted fever in the country, with Virginia not far behind. Sporting a lone white dot on its back, the lone star tick (*Amblyomma americanum*) can transmit a bacterium that causes human ehrlichiosis. Smaller than a sesame seed, the tiny deer tick or blacklegged tick (*Ixodes scapularis*) can transmit organisms responsible for Lyme disease. Be sure to do a tick check daily and remove ticks when found.

CALICO PENNANT
Celithemis elisa
Skimmer family
(Libellulidae)
Quick ID: wings clear with red, orange, and black spots; thorax red with black stripes; eyes red; on abdomen males have bright-red heart-shaped marks, females have yellow marks
Length: 1"–1.3"

The identification of dragonflies and damselflies is a fun but challenging game for budding naturalists. Dragonflies have robust bodies and at rest keep their wings flat out to the sides, like an airplane. Damselflies are slender and generally keep their wings closed above their body when at rest, much like a bird keeps its wings at rest.

RABID WOLF SPIDER
Rabidosa rabida
Wolf spider family
(Lycosidae)
Quick ID: dark brown with grayish markings
Length: body 0.12"–1.4"

Wolf spiders get their name from their wolflike ability to stealthily stalk their insect prey. The rabid wolf spider is a fast and aggressive hunter but is not dangerous to humans. The female carries her newly hatched spiderlings on her back for about a week. Although wolf spiders resemble tarantulas, they are not closely related. The only tarantula in this area is the size of a BB. The spruce fir moss spider (*Microhexura montivaga*) is an endangered species that is found only on the highest peaks in North Carolina and Tennessee. The spider's habitat is suffering due to an infestation by the balsam wooly adelgid (*Adelges piceae*), an introduced pest that is killing Fraser firs.

CAROLINA MANTIS
Stagmomantis carolina
Mantid family (Mantidae)
Quick ID: pale green to brownish gray, light-green wings, triangular head, prominent compound eyes
Length: 2.38"

The Carolina mantis is the state insect of neighboring South Carolina. Uniquely adapted for grasping prey, mantids often hold their elongated forelegs in a cocked position, leading to the common name praying mantis. Voracious carnivores, female mantids will even eat their mates.

ROUND-TIPPED CONEHEAD
Neoconocephalus retusus
Katydid family (Tettigoniidae)
Quick ID: light brown or light green, slanted face, small cone on tip of head
Length: 1.5"–2"

During warm days from midsummer into autumn, the Blue Ridge Parkway is filled with song. The tunes of bluegrass musicians are enriched by the soothing background music of singing insects. These "dog days" of summer are the time when katydids, grasshoppers, crickets, and locusts tune up to advertise their presence to attract a mate. The round-tipped conehead tries his best to join the chorus, but his song is a dry, crackling buzz that sounds like an electronic short.

CRANE FLY
Tipula submaculata
Crane fly family (Tipulidae)
Quick ID: looks like giant mosquito, elongated body, long slender legs, narrow wings
Length: 0.2"-1.9"

With a needlelike body and long legs, the crane fly is an insect that looks like a giant mosquito and is sure to command attention, but crane flies are not mosquitoes at all, and they are totally harmless. Their long dangling legs are similar to those of tall birds called cranes, hence the common name. Important members of the food chain, they are typically found near wet areas where they are nabbed by birds, fish, frogs, and other insects.

MILLIPEDE
Millipede sp.
Polished millipede family (Xystodesmidae)
Quick ID: 2 pairs of legs per segment, often colorful
Length: 1"-5"

Visitors often see these brightly colored multilegged wormlike creatures and mistake them for centipedes. Millipedes have 2 pairs of legs per body segment while centipedes have a single pair of legs for each segment. Centipedes can bite but millipedes cannot. As a defense mechanism, they instead often contain a chemical similar to cyanide that is very distasteful.

Fall Leaf Color ID

Red/Orange	Yellow/Gold	Brown
Black gum	American chestnut	Fraser magnolia
Fetterbush	American elm	Post oak
Flowering dogwood	Beech	River birch
Mountain ash	Black cherry	Sycamore
Poison ivy	Black locust	White oak
Red maple	Black oak	
Red oak	Chestnut oak	
Sassafras	Fringe tree	
Scarlet oak	Grape	
Sourwood	Mountain ash	
Sumac	Pawpaw	
Virginia creeper	Pipe vine	
White ash	Redbud	
White oak	River birch	
	Sassafras	
	Shagbark hickory	
	Spicebush	
	Striped maple	
	Tulip poplar	
	Walnut	
	Witch hazel	

RED MAPLE
Acer rubrum
Maple family (Aceraceae)
Quick ID: opposite leaves, 2"–5" with 3–5 relatively shallow lobes (variable) with red stem, red flower clusters, red winged seeds (samaras)
Height: 20'–40'

Eight of the 13 native species of maples in North America can be found along the Parkway. The abundant red maple provides brilliant red colors in the fall. The leaves of red maple have shallow lobes and a red stem. Silver maple (*A. saccharinum*) is taller, and its silvery-green leaves have 5 deep lobes that turn mostly yellow in the fall. Sugar maple (*A. saccharum*) also has 5 lobed leaves, but they are more moderately notched and are pale green beneath. Similar to sugar maple, the introduced Norway maple (*A. platanoides*) has leaves that are broader with 5 toothed lobes. Also similar to sugar maple, the uncommon black maple (*A. nigrum*) has dark-green 3-lobed leaves that turn yellow in fall.

PAWPAW
Asimina triloba
Custard apple family (Annonaceae)
Quick ID: large 6"–12" oval leaves with parallel veins; greenish-yellow to brown oblong fruit, 4" long
Height: 6'–20'

The lyrics of a traditional American folksong that tells of "picking up pawpaws and put them in your pocket" was sung by children sent to gather the delicious fruits in fall. An uncomely fruit, the pawpaw fruit tastes like a custardy banana and is used in ice creams and pies or eaten raw. Pawpaws were even a favorite of our early presidents George Washington and Thomas Jefferson. Many species of wildlife also enjoy the fruits, including bears, raccoons, squirrels, and opossums, and they are the food plant for zebra swallowtails. The leaves, twigs, and bark contain chemicals that naturally repel insects, and they have been used to fend off lice, fleas, and ticks. Pawpaw seeds are being used in studies as anticancer agents for prostate and colon cancers.

98

FLOWERING DOGWOOD
Cornus florida
Dogwood family (Cornaceae)
Quick ID: rounded top, low spreading branches, greenish-yellow tiny flowers, white bracts, red fruit
Height: 10'–35'

Honoring the lovely flowering dogwood as the state flower of both Virginia and North Carolina may be a bit misleading as the showy white flowers are actually white bracts surrounding tiny greenish-yellow flowers, and it is not a wildflower but actually a small tree. Dogwood trees may have received their common name from England, where people used a bath infused with the bark of the European common dogwood (*C. sanguinea*) to rid their dogs of mange. Another theory about the origin of the common name is from the Old English *dagwood*, derived from the practice of using the hard, slender stems to make daggers and arrows. In 1991 the prehistoric iceman "Ötzi" was discovered in the Italian Alps with arrows made from dogwood.

SOURWOOD
Oxydendrum arboreum
Heath family (Ericaceae)
Quick ID: elliptical finely toothed 4"–8" leaves, deeply furrowed bark, white bell-shaped flowers in clusters
Height: 25'–40'

Sourwood is a prized tree of the Appalachians, loved for its graceful spray of white bell-shaped flowers in spring and its bright colorful leaves in fall. Although the leaves and sap of this native tree have a sour taste, the honey from bees that have nectared on the flowers of sourwood has a uniquely flavorful taste. Sourwood honey has long been used to sweeten foods, and many families gather the honey to sell for extra cash. In fall the leaves of sourwood turn flame red, decorating the forests with brilliant scarlet intensity. Native Americans used the wood to make arrows, pipe stems, and other carvings. White-tailed deer frequently browse on the twigs, and bees and butterflies enjoy the abundant nectar.

BLACK LOCUST
Robinia pseudoacacia
Pea family (Fabaceae)
Quick ID: white clustered flowers, short paired spines along twigs, compound leaves with 7–19 oval leaflets
Height: 70'–80'

In spring the heady fragrance of black locust flowers fills the air along the Parkway, attracting bees and hummingbirds. Black locust is well known as a pioneer species as it establishes quickly and grows well in disturbed areas, effectively helping prevent erosion. Similar in appearance to honey locust, the leaflets of black locust are oval and broader than those of honey locust. Honey locust (*Gleditsia triacanthos*) also possesses wickedly long, unpaired thorns that were used as pins and spear points, while the paired spines of black locust are smaller and stouter. The hard, rot-resistant wood was used to make flooring, furniture, fence posts, and rails. It was also valued as firewood because it burns slowly with little smoke.

EASTERN REDBUD
Cercis canadensis
Pea family (Fabaceae)
Quick ID: heart-shaped leaves, purplish-rose-colored pealike flowers in tufts along the branches
Height: 20'–30'

Even before the leaves unfurl, the rose-colored pealike flowers of redbud emerge in late April and early May in open areas along the Parkway. Redbud is a relatively short, rounded tree with spreading zigzag branches sporting heart-shaped leaves. The flowers are followed by flat 3-inch pods that contain seeds that are eaten by birds and small mammals. Native Americans and settlers added the flowers that are high in vitamin C to salads, and the tender young seed pods were eaten raw or cooked. The twigs were used as a seasoning to cook meats such as venison and opossum. The twigs were also boiled in water to produce a yellow dye.

AMERICAN CHESTNUT
Castanea dentata
Beech family (Fagaceae)
Quick ID: traditionally tall, straight; at this time grows only from shoots; flowers—long creamy white upright catkins; fruit—nuts in spiny seed pods; leaves—narrow, coarsely toothed, 4"–8" long, 2"–3" wide, tapering to a point
Height: 60'–80'

Dominating the forests of Appalachia, in the early 1900s the mighty American chestnut met its demise from the gripping strangle of a tiny fungus. Chestnuts were integral to life in Appalachia, where the straight, rot-resistant lumber was used for homes, furniture, barns, and fences. The sweet nuts were made into breads, puddings, and soups, and the leaves were used as a remedy for rheumatism, colds, and whooping cough. The fungus, *Cryphonectria parasitica*, was spread from imported trees, and by 1930 most populations of chestnut were destroyed. The plants still send up shoots but are infected before producing seeds. Efforts are under way by groups such as the American Chestnut Foundation to restore this magnificent tree to the Appalachian forests.

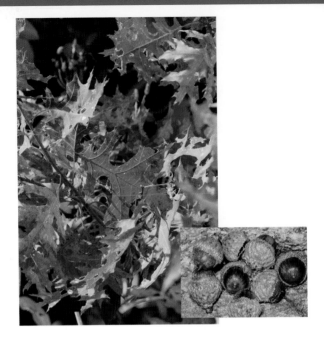

SCARLET OAK
Quercus coccinea
Beech family (Fagaceae)
Quick ID: glossy alternate leaves with deep C-shaped sinuses, bark with broad irregular ridges and narrow furrows
Height: 60'–80'

A medium-size tree of dry rocky slopes and ridges, scarlet oak is best known for its brilliant addition to the kaleidoscope of fall colors. It occurs at middle and lower elevations in the Appalachians up to about 5,000 feet. Cherished for its intense scarlet leaves in autumn, it is also widely planted as a fast-growing shade tree. The cap on the acorns covers about half of the nut, and the tip of the nut may have concentric rings. Many forest animals depend on the nuts as an important food source; this includes white-tailed deer, squirrels, and chipmunks. Several bird species such as wild turkey, blue jays, and woodpeckers eat the nuts.

YELLOW BUCKEYE
Aesculus flava
Horse-chestnut family (Hippocastanaceae)
Quick ID: straight, tall, leaves palmlike with 5 oval saw-edged leaflets each 3"–7" long, light-grayish-brown platelike bark
Height: 50'–75'

A common and characteristic tree, yellow buckeye is a native tree that grows in rich, moist southern Appalachian forests. In April and May creamy yellow blossoms appear in showy upright clusters about 6 inches above the graceful branches. The large palm-shaped leaves are divided into 5 oval, toothed leaflets that provide ample shade from the hot summer sun, and the trees were often planted in yards to act as a giant living umbrella. Thick, leathery husks enclose 1 to 3 shiny brown seeds. A buckeye seed was often carried in a trouser pocket as a good luck charm thought to prevent rheumatism. Native Americans used the straight wood for furniture, baby cradles, and to make ceremonial masks.

BLACK WALNUT
Juglans nigra
Walnut family (Juglandaceae)
Quick ID: 12"–24" leaves with 15–23 narrow leaflets, dark bark with diamond-shaped furrows, round green husk covering wrinkled brown nut
Height: 70'–100'

The long 18-inch leaf of the walnut tree has numerous narrow, toothed leaflets, with the terminal leaflet typically small or absent. Similar trees are butternut (*J. cinerea*), which has oval fruits, and tree-of-heaven (*Ailanthus altissima*), but the leaflets of this nonnative are notched at the base. An exceptionally valuable tree, the walnut is revered for its delicious nuts as well as its superior hardwood, which is used in a variety of wood products. Early hunters prized the strong wood for making essential gunstocks that would not warp out of alignment. Skilled cabinetmakers fashioned the velvety dark wood into chairs, bedroom suites, and bookcases. In Appalachian kitchens walnuts were an important ingredient in many recipes for cakes, cookies, and candies.

SHAGBARK HICKORY
Carya ovata
Walnut family (Juglandaceae)
Quick ID: 8"–14" compound leaf with 5 pointed leaflets; 1.5"–3" egg-shaped nuts; light, shaggy bark
Height: 60'–90'

Along with oaks, hickories are one of the most common trees in the forests along the Blue Ridge Parkway. Hickories have compound leaves typically with 5 pointed leaflets. Several species of this tall tree are found along the Parkway, including shagbark, bitternut, pignut, and mockernut hickory. Hickories are members of the walnut family and produce nuts that are consumed by many species of wildlife including squirrels, turkeys, and black bears. The sweet nuts were also an important staple for Native Americans and early settlers. The strong, heavy wood was used for tool handles, furniture, gunstocks, and barrel hoops as well as firewood for heating and cooking.

SASSAFRAS
Sassafras albidum
Laurel family (Lauraceae)
Quick ID: small- to medium-size tree, leaves variable with 2 or 3 lobes or unlobed
Height: 10'–50'

Sassafras is a common small tree that grows in open areas along the Parkway, especially in fields and along forest edges. The nickname "mitten tree" gives a clue to the unusual shape of some of the leaves of sassafras, which often resemble small mittens. All parts of this tree are spicy scented; in fact the roots and bark were used to flavor root beer until 1960. In the early 1600s sassafras was one of the first forest products exported to England. Southerners dried the leaves and ground them into a powder known as filé powder that they used for thickening soups, sauces, and gumbos. In fall the leaves turn yellow and orange, and birds enjoy the dark-blue berries, while white-tailed deer browse the twigs.

FRASER MAGNOLIA
Magnolia fraseri
Magnolia family (Magnoliaceae)
Quick ID: large 8"–18" diamond-shaped leaves broadest beyond middle, 5"–8" wide, 2 "ear" lobes at base; large creamy-white flowers with 6–9 petals; red fruit
Height: 30'–70'

Magnolias are one of the oldest-known families of trees, with fossil evidence indicating that they were abundant during the Cretaceous and Tertiary periods. The creamy-white lotus-like blossoms have 6 to 9 petals, and the 10-inch-long leaves are lobed at the base. The fruit is rose red and is produced on a cone-like seed-bearing structure about 3.5 inches long. Each seed has a bright-red fleshy outer layer called an aril. Two other magnolias can regularly be seen along the Parkway. The larger 12- to 24-inch-long leaves of umbrella magnolia (*M. tripetala*) lack the earlobes at the base of the leaf. The cucumber magnolia (*M. acuminata*) has smaller, 6- to 10-inch-long oval leaves without the earlobes.

TULIP TREE
Liriodendron tulipifera
Magnolia family (Magnoliaceae)
Quick ID: tall, straight trunk, tulip-shaped yellow-orange flowers, smooth leaves with 4–6 lobes
Height: 50'–100'

Tulip poplar and yellow poplar are 2 alternate names for the tulip tree due to the resemblance of its quaking leaves and light-colored wood to that of true poplars. In spring the showy, yellowish-orange flowers look like tulips or lilies growing high in the canopy. The flowers provide nectar for bees that make a dark, strong-tasting honey that was gathered by settlers for use in baking. Native Americans hollowed out the tall, straight trunks to fashion into canoes and cradles. During the Civil War the bark of tulip tree was mixed with willow bark as a remedy for various fevers of soldiers. Their horses were also medicated with the powdered bark as a tonic.

FRINGE TREE
Chionanthus virginicus
Olive family (Oleaceae)
Quick ID: creamy-white drooping feathery flowers, opposite oval leaves, dark-blue oval fruits
Height: 12'–20'

In May the heady sweet orange-blossom perfume from the feathery white flowers of fringe tree fills the evening air in quiet forest edges along the Parkway. In the same family as ash trees, forsythia, lilac, and jasmines, fringe tree grows best in partial shade and moist areas and is often planted as an ornamental tree much valued for its intoxicating fragrance in spring. In late summer the small tree produces abundant dark-blue jellybean-size fruits that are relished by birds such as gray catbirds and brown thrashers.

WHITE ASH
Fraxinus americana
Olive family (Oleaceae)

Quick ID: opposite compound leaves with 5–9 leaflets, lower surface of leaflets pale green
Height: 70'–80'

Due to its strength and flexibility, ash is one of the best woods for making chairs and other furniture. It is also used almost exclusively in the production of wooden baseball bats. An important wood for settlers, it was carved into handles for hoes, shovels, axes, knives, and other essential tools. Used in folk remedies, the crushed leaves were carried in a pocket to prevent rattlesnake bites. The juice from the leaves was also used to relieve the itch of mosquito bites. The emerald ash borer (*Agrilus planipennis*), an invasive wood-boring beetle accidentally introduced in the 1990s, is destroying ash trees throughout the United States and Canada, where efforts are under way to halt its spread.

PRINCESS TREE
Paulownia tomentosa
Paulownia family (Paulowniaceae)
Quick ID: paired 6"–13" heart-shaped leaves that are hairy below; lavender trumpet-shaped clusters of flowers; winged seeds in dry, brown 4-sided capsules
Height: 30'–60'

Introduced from Asia in the early 1800s, princess tree was planted as a fast-growing wood for export purposes. The tree thrived and spread throughout the eastern United States, where it grows rapidly in disturbed areas such as roadsides, stream banks, and forest edges, quickly outcompeting native trees. In spring the showy lavender trumpet-shaped flowers fill the air with a pleasing vanilla scent. Winged seeds are formed in a 4-sided dry, brown, pecan-shaped capsule. Princess trees, which are also known as empress trees or royal paulownias, are sometimes confused with catalpa trees, which have cigar-shaped seedpods. Now placed in its own family, Paulowniaceae, the name honors Anna Pavlovna (Paulowna) (1795–1865), daughter of Tsar Paul I of Russia.

CAROLINA HEMLOCK
Tsuga caroliniana
Pine family (Pinaceae)
Quick ID: compact pyramid-shaped evergreen; short, flattened, diamond-shaped needles arranged like a bottlebrush
Height: 40'–60'

Endemic to the southern Appalachians, the Carolina hemlock is found on partly shaded rocky hillsides. Spreading in all directions around the stems, the glossy needles resemble green plastic bottlebrushes. Also found along the Parkway, the more common eastern hemlock, *T. canadensis,* has longer needles that are arranged more or less in a flat plane. Both species are prone to invasion by the introduced hemlock wooly adelgid, a devastating scale insect that destroys these beautiful trees. Native Americans used the bark to make a rosy-tan dye, and the pliable inner bark was used to make baskets. Look for Carolina hemlock in the Linville Gorge area, at Chestoa View Overlook in areas near Pisgah National Forest.

FRASER FIR
Abies fraseri
Pine family (Pinaceae)
Quick ID: silvery evergreen with pointed crown; gray-brown bark with resin blisters; curved needles at right angles, dark green above, chalky white below; 1.5"–2.5" erect cones
Height: 30'–50'

Well known as a favorite evergreen tree, the Fraser fir is locally grown on the hillsides of North Carolina Christmas tree farms. In the wild Fraser fir is restricted to high elevations of the southern Appalachians including North Carolina and Virginia. With its shiny flat needles, Fraser fir is locally known as "she-balsam" while red spruce (*Picea rubens*) with prickly needles is known as "he-balsam." The tree is named to honor the Scottish botanist John Fraser, who researched plant life of the Appalachians around 1800. Sometimes called balsam fir, look for Fraser fir growing along high altitude trails such as those at Richland Balsam. An introduced aphid-like insect, the balsam woolly adelgid, *Adelges piceae*, is attacking this species.

WHITE PINE
Pinus strobus
Pine family (Pinaceae)
Quick ID: tall evergreen, 4" needles in bundles of 5, bark with deep furrows, 5.5" cones slender and tapered toward the end are often dotted with sap
Height: 80'–110'

Five trees in the pine genus can be found along the Parkway, but white pine is one of the most recognizable as it is often sold for use as Christmas trees. Along the graceful horizontal branches, the needles form clusters with 5 needles. Early colonists used white pines as ship masts, and the pine resin was used to waterproof baskets and wooden pails. Pitch pine (*P. rigida*), another pine that can be found along the Parkway, has needles in bundles of 3, which often grow directly out of the trunk. The other pines found here include Virginia pine (*P. virginiana*), Table Mountain pine (*P. pungens*), and shortleaf pine (*P. echinata*), each of which has 2 needles per bundle.

SYCAMORE
Platanus occidentalis
Plane-tree family (Platanaceae)
Quick ID: massive tree, tan bark peels off in sheets to reveal white underneath, heavy spreading branches, broad maplelike leaves with notched lobes, ball of seeds
Height: 50'–130'

The majestic sycamore is one of the most common trees found along rivers, streams, and wetlands. Soaring over its neighbors, the sycamore can reach 130 feet tall, providing delightfully cool shade on hot summer days. The characteristic camouflage tan-and-white bark pattern results in older trees because, unlike most trees, the bark of the sycamore does not have the ability to expand as it grows. Native Americans used sycamore for a variety of medicinal purposes including coughs, sores, and urinary and reproductive ailments. The strong yellowish wood was used as furniture, chopping blocks, and particularly as buttons, which led to the common name "buttonwood."

ALLEGHENY SERVICEBERRY
Amelanchier laevis
Rose family (Rosaceae)
Quick ID: small tree or shrub; showy star-shaped white flower; purplish fruits; alternate smooth, oval leaves with fine serrations
Height: 10'–40'

In April and May a view from the Parkway into the valleys and hillsides appears as if nature has hung out the linens to freshen them in the warm spring breeze as the bright white flowers of Allegheny serviceberry dot the leafless landscape. One of the first trees to flower in spring, the Allegheny serviceberry is known by many other names, including smooth service-berry, referring to the smooth leaves. The berries appear in June, hence another common name, Juneberry. Shad ran in the rivers at the same time the blooms appeared, hence "shadbush" or "shadblow." Early settlers knew that when the "sarvisberry" bloomed, the preacher could make it into the mountains for a church service, or in mountain dialect, "sarvis."

APPLE
Malus pumila
Rose family (Rosaceae)
Quick ID: pinkish-white flowers with 5 rounded petals; finely toothed oval leaves; stout, twisted trunk
Height: 20'–30'

In May pink apple blossoms burst from their buds, promising a fruitful harvest in fall. Many families along the Blue Ridge still depend on apples as an important crop for economic and domestic use. Historically, settlers and their families worked hard to clear and plant hillsides full of apple trees. Varieties such as Grimes Golden, Aunt Rachel, Horse Apple, Newtown Pippin, Jonathan, and Winesap were once widely grown. Passionate about apples, textile entrepreneur Moses Cone grew 75 different varieties of apple on 10,000 apple trees in orchards that he planted on the rolling hills surrounding Flat Top Manor. Along the Parkway at MP 328.3, the Orchard at Altapass (a nonprofit organization) offers visitors a unique view into the traditional culture of apples.

119

BLACK CHERRY
Prunus serotina
Rose family (Rosaceae)
Quick ID: white drooping flowers on stalk; shiny oblong, finely toothed leaves; dark-red fruit
Height: 60'–80'

Recognized as one of the most important wild trees, the black cherry is a valuable resource for wild animals, birds, and humans. While the fruit is edible, the rest of the plant can be toxic, which is of special concern to farmers whose cattle may eat the wilted leaves. Black bears are especially fond of the ripe cherries and in the fall can be found gorging on the delicious treats. The wood was especially favored by colonial furniture makers for rocking chairs, spindle beds, and other fine furniture. Cherries were gathered for jellies and pies and were also made into wines and cordials. The inner bark was used in cough syrups and as a sedative.

MOUNTAIN ASH
Sorbus americana
Rose family (Rosaceae)
Quick ID: compound leaves, 11–17 pointed-toothed leaflets, bright-red berries
Height: 15'–30'

Mountain ash is best known for its clusters of fire-engine-red berries, which it produces in the fall. Actually a member of the rose family, mountain ash is not related to ash trees, but it does have similar-looking leaves. Although the bright-red berries are very tart, after a frost they sweeten and were used by early settlers to make jellies and wines and were cooked with meat. Many birds, such as American robins, cedar waxwings, and juncos, gorge themselves on the ripe berries in fall. White-tailed deer browse on the leaves and twigs. You can see mountain ash along the Parkway at Craggy Gardens Visitor Center, Mount Pisgah Lodge, and along the Richland Balsam Trail.

ELDERBERRY
Sambucus canadensis
Moschatel family (Adoxaceae)
Quick ID: opposite compound 6"–11" leaves, 5–9 toothed leaflets; creamy-white flowers in broad, dense, flat-topped clusters; blackish-blue fruits
Height: 3'–13'

To Southerners, elderberry is a source of delightful food and drinks. The large plate-size clusters of creamy-white flowers in spring would eventually fade into handfuls of juicy blue-black berries. Long used medicinally, parts of the plant have been used as a remedy for colds, flu, fevers, constipation, and skin conditions. The plant contains a chemical similar to cyanide and can be toxic. Eating uncooked or unripe berries can cause diarrhea or vomiting. Cooking the berries makes them safe to eat, and they are prized for use in pies, jellies, pancakes, syrups, and wine. Elderberries are high in vitamins A and C, and they contain more cancer-fighting antioxidants than blueberries or cranberries.

122

HOBBLEBUSH
Viburnum lantanoides
Moschatel family (Adoxaceae)
Quick ID: white flowers in flat-topped clusters; 4"–8"-long heart-shaped, finely toothed leaves; dark-purple fruits
Height: 6'–10'

As the branches of hobblebush, or witch hobble as it is sometimes called, bend and take root along the ground, they form loops that may trip or "hobble" unwary hikers. The large clusters of creamy-white, flat-topped flowers attract insects and butterflies and are the larval host for the spring azure butterfly. Formally known as *Viburnum alnifolium,* this and all other viburnums have been removed from the honeysuckle family, Caprifoliaceae, and are now placed in the Moschatel family called Adoxaceae. Found in cool, moist woods, this is one of the earliest of spring bloomers. Hobblebush contains antifreeze agents that help its leaves withstand temperatures to –23°F, making it one of the most cold tolerant of all woody plants.

STAGHORN SUMAC
Rhus typhina
Sumac family (Anacardiaceae)
Quick ID: hairy twigs and leafstalks, 15"-long compound leaves, 11–31 pointed 3.5" leaflets, reddish berries in 6" clusters
Height: 4'–15'

All 3 species of sumac found along the Parkway have long compound leaves and clusters of reddish berries in fall. The lemony berries were once commonly used to make a refreshing summer drink and were given to children to stop bed-wetting. The stems of staghorn sumac are covered in hairs reminiscent of the antlers of a buck "in velvet." Smooth sumac (*R. glabra*) lacks the hairs of staghorn sumac. Winged sumac (*R. copallinum*), also known as flameleaf or shining sumac, has shiny green leaflets with the leaf midrib (rachis) bordered by thin leafy "wings." Poison sumac (*Toxicodendron vernix*) is found only in swampy and coastal areas of Virginia and North Carolina.

WINTERBERRY HOLLY
Ilex montana
Holly family (Aquifoliaceae)
Quick ID: alternate oval, slightly toothed deciduous leaves; tiny white flowers; reddish berries
Height: 20'–30'

Many holly species are evergreen with shiny spiked leaves that remain throughout the winter. The leaves of this member of the holly family are deciduous, falling off in fall to leave the bright red berries behind from which the name winterberry holly derives. This large shrub is sometimes characterized as a small tree and is common in the forest understory. Also called mountain holly or mountain winterberry, it is one of about 10 native hollies in the southern Appalachian mountains. The reddish berries, or drupes, often hang on the branches into winter and are a valuable food source for wildlife. The fruits are eaten by many birds including blue jays, cedar waxwings, eastern bluebirds, American robins, and wild turkeys.

COMMON SWEETSHRUB
Calycanthus floridus
Strawberry shrub family (Calycanthaceae)
Quick ID: opposite leathery oval leaves, flower with numerous dark rusty-reddish-brown
overlapping petals
Height: 4'–7'

Blooming from May through July, the unusual dark-reddish-brown
wooden-looking flowers of sweetshrub are often overlooked. With a
strawberry-bubblegum scent, they are sometimes smelled before they are
seen. The oil from the flowers is used in perfumes. The shrub is often
planted in yards as a fragrant ornamental. Generally insect- and disease-
free, it contains an alkaloid similar to strychnine called calycanthine and
is toxic to most animals.

MOUNTAIN SWEET PEPPERBUSH
Clethra acuminata
Clethra family (Clethraceae)
Quick ID: multiple stems, peeling reddish-brown bark, drooping spikes of white flowers
Height: 8'–12'

Mountain sweet pepperbush is a large shrub endemic to the southern Appalachian Mountains. In mid-July the tiny white bell-shaped fragrant flowers appear on 6-inch spikes that gracefully wave in the breeze. The strikingly beautiful cinnamon-colored bark peels away in sheets, giving rise to the common name cinnamon clethra. Used medicinally, Native Americans mixed the bark with wild cherry bark to prepare a decoction to give to patients with high fever. Early settlers used the spicy seeds as a substitute for black pepper.

CAROLINA RHODODENDRON
Rhododendron carolinianum
Heath family (Ericaceae)
Quick ID: 2"–3" glossy dark-green leaves, clusters of 5–10 pink flowers
Height: 3'–5'

A smaller version of the pink rhododendron, Carolina rhododendron is not as commonly seen as its larger relatives. The delicate light-pink flowers bloom in mid-May, before most of the larger rhododendrons. Bees and other flying insects pollinate the blooms. The glossy evergreen leaves remain on the shrub through the winter. Carolina rhododendron has been taxonomically separated from the closely related gorge rhododendron (*R. minus*), which grows in the Piedmont and coastal plain. Carolina rhododendron is a southern Appalachian endemic found at high altitudes along the Parkway from the Linville Gorge area south and west to the Great Smoky Mountains.

CATAWBA RHODODENDRON
Rhododendron catawbiense
Heath family (Ericaceae)
Quick ID: deep-pink large flower 5" across, 3"–6" oblong evergreen leaves
Height: 6'–10'

June is a wonderful time to visit the Blue Ridge Parkway as one of the most spectacular shows of wildflowers bursts forth with a stunning display. The show begins in late May to mid-June with the awe-inspiring deep-pink blooms of Catawba rhododendron lining the Parkway and creating a sea of pink through which motorists pass. Spring festivals abound, including the Roan Mountain Rhododendron Festival held in Roan Mountain State Park, TN 20 west of Banner Elk, North Carolina. You can also spy the rhododendron displays at Mount Rogers, which is the highest mountain in Virginia. Along the Parkway you can enjoy a hike at Craggy Gardens, where the trail leads through a natural tunnel of the pink flowers.

DOG HOBBLE
Leucothoe fontanesiana
Heath family (Ericaceae)
Quick ID: tiny white bell-shaped flowers, leathery dark-green leaves with fine serrations, small white bell-shaped flowers in fragrant clusters
Height: 3'–6'

The arching branches, dark leathery leaves, and fragrant white bell-shaped flowers of dog hobble make this shrub one of the most graceful shrubs in the mountains. The arching stems bend toward the ground, forming suckers that colonize the area. They become so dense that they make it difficult for hunting dogs and humans to pass through, hence the name dog hobble. Also known as mountain leucothoe, the genus obtained its name from a Greek myth. Leucothoe was the daughter of a Persian king who fell in love with Helios, the god who drove the chariot of horses that pulled the sun across the sky. When Helios tried to sneak into her room, her father was so angry that he buried her alive.

FLAME AZALEA
Rhododendron calendulaceum
Heath family (Ericaceae)
Quick ID: orange funnel-shaped flowers with 5 spreading lobes, 1"–3"-long oval leaves
Height: 6'–10'

A showstopper of the plant world, the blooms of flame azalea explode with bright-orange color into the spring tango of fresh green leaves and vivid blue skies. The color is so intense that when visitors see them, they look like bright fires burning on the hillsides. In May or early June, the 2-inch-long vase-shaped flowers, which vary from bright red-orange to pale orangish yellow, attract bees, butterflies, and hummingbirds with their blooms. The stamens of the flower protrude like long, arching antennae eager to brush pollen on these visitors. You can see flame azalea at Whetstone Ridge and Craggy Gardens Visitor Center.

GREAT RHODODENDRON
Rhododendron maximum
Heath family (Ericaceae)
Quick ID: 3"–14" large leathery oblong leaves with rolled edges, flowers white with pink-ish tinge and usually some green dots
Height: 10'–30'

Great rhododendron is locally known as "rosebay rhododendron," "great laurel," or more commonly, "laurel." It is one of the most common rhododendrons in the southern Appalachians, with thickets of dense plants following streams and filling rich coves with their characteristic pink-tinged white blooms. The leaves are somewhat hairy and whitish underneath. The dominant understory plant on millions of acres, the dense thickets have been shown to reduce the species diversity of other plants. Although bloom times vary from year to year, depending on elevation, most plants start blooming in late June as the blooms of the other rhododendrons are fading away. The Mabry Mill area is a good place to see these lovely evergreen shrubs at their best.

MOUNTAIN FETTERBUSH
Pieris floribunda
Heath family (Ericaceae)
Quick ID: small white urn-shaped flowers in upright clusters, alternate leaves finely toothed, oval evergreen, pale shiny green above, yellow-green underneath
Height: 3'–6'

Mountain fetterbush is a southern Appalachian endemic common at high elevations in the North Carolina mountains. The tiny white urn-shaped flowers bloom in early spring, then leave behind green capsules that dry and turn brown. Very similar to mountain laurel, the bark is gray and peeling on branches that are thickly matted, binding or fettering the feet of anyone trying to pass through. Grouse and other small animals find protection and shelter in the branches. The white flowers are shaped like triangular upside-down urns with ridges. Fetterbush Overlook at MP 421.7 is in a mountainous area where these small shrubs are often seen growing on rocky, exposed areas. The leaves are highly toxic and may be fatal if eaten.

MOUNTAIN LAUREL
Kalmia latifolia
Heath family (Ericaceae)
Quick ID: 2"–5" leathery pointed evergreen leaves, bowl-shaped pink flowers
Height: 6'–10'

Pastel-pink saucer-shaped flowers of mountain laurel bloom in May and June along the Parkway. Known locally as "ivy," mountain laurel is an evergreen shrub that forms thickets of impenetrable gnarly branches. These dense patches are locally known as "laurel hells" or "ivy thickets." If you look closely at the flowers, you will notice that the anthers are held in a curved backward arch by 2 small clasps. A visiting bee triggers the release of the anther, catapulting pollen onto the unsuspecting pollinator. Containing the eggs of a scale insect (*Coccidae* sp.), white-fringed black dots can be found under the leaves. Chickadees, kinglets, and other insect-eating birds feed on these stored eggs through the long winter months.

PINXTER AZALEA
Rhododendron periclymenoides
Heath family (Ericaceae)
Quick ID: clusters of pale-pink tubular flowers with long, protruding stamens, 2"–4"
oval leaves
Height: 6'–12'

Along with Carolina rhododendron, pinxter azalea, or pinxter flower, is
one of the earliest rhododendrons to bloom along the Parkway. The 5
long, protruding stamens and one pistil in the large pink funnel-shaped
flowers are characteristic of this deciduous shrub. The flowers attract
butterflies such as the eastern tiger swallowtail. The name "pinxter"
comes from the Dutch word for Pentecost, not for its pink coloration.
Supposedly, this plant was in bloom during this holiday. Large pale-green
galls caused by a fungus called *Exobasidium vaccinii* are common on the
branch tips and leaves of pinxter flower. The galls, called mayapples or
honeysuckle apples, were once pickled and eaten.

BRISTLY LOCUST
Robinia hispida
Pea family (Fabaceae)
Quick ID: shrub, pink flowers, bristly pods, leaves compound with 9–13 leaflets
Height: 2'–10'

Most noticeable in spring, the pinkish-rose-colored flowers hang in lavish clusters from this shrub that grows along roads or the edges of fields. Forming thickets from root sprouts, the stems and branches of bristly locust are covered with reddish-golden bristly hairs. Bristly locust is native to the Appalachians but has spread due to cultivation. In midsummer the leaflets often have brown fingerlike blotches called a "mine" due to a small moth caterpillar (*Parectopa robiniella*) that burrows through the leaf. The silver-spotted skipper butterfly lays its eggs on the leaves of bristly locust and black locust. After emerging, the colorful green caterpillars chew the midvein of the leaflets to form a tent for protection while feasting on the foliage.

WITCH HAZEL
Hamamelis virginiana
Witch-hazel family (Hamamelidaceae)
Quick ID: wavy-toothed leaves, yellow flowers in late fall
Height: 10'–25'

An oddity among the plant world, the straggly yellow flowers of witch hazel do not bloom until late fall, often after the first snowfall. It blooms about the same time as the dry seedpods open up and audibly eject the small seeds with a loud "pop" up to 20 feet from the plant. After steeping the bark and leaves in water, early settlers used the liquid to relieve itching from mosquitoes, chiggers, and poison ivy. Some people, called "dowsers" or "water witchers," used a forked stem of witch hazel to "divine" the underground location of water. Holding the forked portion with both hands, they walked until the end of the stick began to bob and twitch, declaring the location of water.

WILD HYDRANGEA
Hydrangea arborescens
Hydrangea family (Hydrangeaceae)
Quick ID: opposite serrated heart-shaped leaves, flat-topped clusters of small white flowers
Height: 3'–6'

Commonly known as wild hydrangea or smooth hydrangea, this medium-size shrub is native to the eastern United States. The familiar cultivated hydrangeas typically have sterile flowers, but the clusters of tiny white flowers are mostly fertile in wild hydrangea. Native Americans used wild hydrangea in a variety of ways. The new growth of young twigs was cooked and eaten like green beans, and the peeled branches and twigs were boiled to make into a tea. An infusion of the bark was used for sick children and to induce vomiting. The bark was chewed for high blood pressure and stomach troubles. They also scraped the bark to be used as a poultice for burns, sprains, and sore muscles.

SPICEBUSH
Lindera benzoin
Laurel family (Lauraceae)
Quick ID: alternate simple 4" leaves, small yellow flowers in clusters, red berrylike fruit
Height: 6'–12'

Even before the leaves come out, the pleasing yellow blossoms of spicebush brighten early spring forests. When rubbed, the leaves and twigs of this shrub produce a spicy aromatic scent. The stems and leaves were once used to brew a spicy tea and were added to roasts of wild game such as opossum or groundhog. Woodland birds such as wood thrush and veery eat the glossy red berrylike fruits called drupes. Spicebush swallowtail butterflies and promethea silk moths lay their eggs on the leaves of spicebush and sassafras. The caterpillars fold the leaves over them tent-fashion for protection when they are not feeding.

YELLOWROOT
Xanthorhiza simplicissima
Buttercup family (Ranunculaceae)
Quick ID: compound leaves spirally arranged on thin stems, small star-shaped purplish flowers with 5 petals
Height: 1'–3'

With its woody stem, yellowroot is a unique member of the Buttercup family. Yellowroot is a small shrub that is native to the eastern United States. The name refers to the yellow roots that were used by Native Americans to make a yellow dye. Yellowroot usually grows by streams and propagates by producing seeds as well as sending out runners. The plant is used in folk medicine for mouth sores, stomach ulcers, and diabetes. It contains berberine, which can stimulate uterine activity (but should not be used during pregnancy). Other potential concerns with its use include its ability to stimulate heart activity and interfere with blood-thinning medications.

MULTIFLORA ROSE
Rosa multiflora
Rose family (Rosaceae)
Quick ID: clusters of 5 white flattened petals on arching stems, 7–9 toothed leaflets, red fruit
Height: 6'–15'

The heady fragrance of wild roses often fills the air in summer, but with 5 flattened white petals, the flowers of multiflora rose do not look much like the cultivated roses that are sold in flower shops. Introduced from Asia in the 1860s as rootstock for ornamental roses, the hardy shrub sends out long-arching stems that easily root themselves quickly into a thicket of thorny brambles. So well did these plants grow that they were utilized as living fences and to prevent erosion on banks. The plant thrived in many types of soil and is now considered a noxious weed in many states. High in vitamin C, the red fruits, called "hips," are used to make jellies and teas.

141

PURPLE FLOWERING RASPBERRY
Rubus odoratus
Rose family (Rosaceae)
Quick ID: rose-purple flower with 5 petals, large maplelike leaves, thornless, bristly hairs on stems, red flattened berries
Height: 3'–6'

Forming large patches of rambling stems, purple flowering raspberry, or flowering raspberry, bushes often cover disturbed areas and open hillsides. Unlike similar berry plants, the leaves of this common shrub are 5-lobed and maplelike, large rather than the compound leaves typically found on other berry bushes. The fruits that appear in late summer are flattened, reddish, and fuzzy. Although the fruits lack the distinctive taste of other berries, they were once used to make jelly and were eaten fresh. The roots were used medicinally by Native Americans for coughs, toothaches, boils, and diarrhea.

SMOOTH BLACKBERRY
Rubus canadensis
Rose family (Rosaceae)
Quick ID: smooth arching stems, alternate leaves, 3–5 toothed leaflets, white flowers with 5 petals, black berries
Height: 6'–10'

In late summer on early mountain farms, one of the chores for children was blackberry picking, which had its good and bad factors. The good part was enjoying the jolting burst of popping a freshly picked berry into your mouth. The bad parts were the prickles and the wildlife (such as bears) that also enjoyed the fresh fruits. The blackberries were used to make scrumptious cobblers, pies, and jams and were sometimes sold to local stores and restaurants. More than 10 related species of berries can be found along the Parkway. Smooth blackberry is found at high elevations and is one of the few blackberry species without prickles. Birds, chipmunks, and squirrels eat the fruits, while deer and rabbits browse the leaves and stems.

POISON IVY
Toxicodendron radicans
Sumac family (Anacardiaceae)
Quick ID: 3 leaflets with pointed tips each 2"–4.5" long, climbing vine, training vine, or shrub

An important plant to get to know, poison ivy contains urushiol, an oil that causes a skin reaction in 80 percent of people. Poison ivy can appear as a trailing vine 4 to 10 inches tall. It can also take the form of a shrub up to 4 feet tall. It may also form a climbing vine resembling a fuzzy rope that grows up to 150 feet on trees. Folk remedies such as pouring bleach on the rash, eating the leaves, or rubbing the leaves on the rash actually may cause more harm. Wash the affected area with cool water and remember the saying "leaves of 3, let it be."

DUTCHMAN'S PIPE
Isotrema macrophyllum
Dutchman's-pipe family (Aristolochiaceae)
Quick ID: woody vine, large 6"–10" heart-shaped leaves, brownish-purple pipe-shaped flowers

Although it is the large heart-shaped leaves that are first noticed on this high-climbing vine, it is the pipe-shaped flowers hidden beneath the leaves that give this vine the common name Dutchman's pipe or pipevine. The Latin name was recently changed from *Aristolochia macrophylla* to *Isotrema macrophyllum*. Used as an aid in childbirth and more recently as a diet aid, a newly discovered ill-fated side effect is that ingestion causes kidney cancer due to a lethal toxin called aristolochic acid. When eating the leaves, pipevine swallowtail caterpillars incorporate the poison into their bodies, providing them an evil-tasting protection from predators. An old-fashioned favorite, pipevine was often planted near porches as its large leaves provided cool shade.

TRUMPET CREEPER
Campsis radicans
Trumpet-creeper family (Bignoniaceae)
Quick ID: red-orange tubular flowers, opposite oval-toothed leaflets, woody vine to 35'

Garlands of tropical red-orange flowers against a background of twining green foliage decorate many garden fences of homes along the Parkway. The 2- to 3-inch-long trumpet-shaped flowers attract ruby-throated hummingbirds, which spread the pollen as they travel from one flower to the next. Climbing by aerial roots, the leaves can cause skin irritation leading to the common name "cow itch."

TRUMPET HONEYSUCKLE
Lonicera sempervirens
Honeysuckle family (Caprifoliaceae)
Quick ID: red tubular flowers in whorled clusters, opposite rounded leaves, red berries

Nature's design is perfect. It has to be or it wouldn't work. All life depends on plants, and since plants are immobile, they depend on pollinators to come to them. The long tubular flowers of trumpet honeysuckle are fire-engine red for a purpose. They are so colored to attract a particular pollinator: the hummingbird. These tiny birds learn that red tubular flowers produce nectar and will favor these over other flowers. As the hummingbird delves into the flower for a nectar reward, the pollen is rubbed onto its head by the perfectly placed anthers. When the hummingbird flies off to the next trumpet honeysuckle flower, it inadvertently rubs the pollen onto the exposed stigma, thus completing the cycle.

ORIENTAL BITTERSWEET
Celastrus orbiculatus
Bittersweet family (Celastraceae)
Quick ID: twining woody stem 30' or longer, orange berries with yellow case at end of twigs, alternate oval leaves with elongated tip

American bittersweet (*C. scandens*) was once gathered for fall decorations and flower arrangements, but this practice has caused a sharp decline in the populations of the vine and is now discouraged. The native American bittersweet is being outcompeted by the introduced oriental bittersweet, which is now one of the most invasive plants in North America. Oriental bittersweet has bright-orange fruits along the entire length of the vine. Birds are attracted to the fruits and play a role in dispersing the seeds. All parts of the plant are poisonous—ingestion of the berries causes vomiting, diarrhea, and in severe cases loss of consciousness. Used medicinally, Native Americans used bittersweet to ease the pain of childbirth.

BEAKED DODDER
Cuscuta rostrata
Morning glory family (Convolvulaceae)
Quick ID: thin whitish to yellowish-orange vine encircling other plants, tiny bell-shaped white flowers, scalelike leaves

Often arousing the curiosity of hikers, dodder is a parasitic plant that is often described as long strands of thin yellow spaghetti. This curious plant is totally dependent on other plants for its nourishment, as it does not produce its own chlorophyll. Dodder sends out tendrils that cling to another plant and encircle it counterclockwise. It then presses little bumps called haustoria into the host plant that allow it to leach out nutrients that it needs to survive. Locals have created many colorful common names to describe this plant including love vine, witch's shoestrings, witch's hair, strangle weed, and devil's hair. The genus *Cuscuta* contains more than 100 species, which are very difficult to identify without a hand lens or microscope.

KUDZU
Pueraria montana var. *lobata*
Pea family (Fabaceae)
Quick ID: 35'–100' climbing vine; 3-lobed leaves; purple flowers; brown, hairy, flattened seed pods

Native to Japan and southeast China, kudzu was first introduced to the United States in 1876 and was planted to reduce soil erosion and as a livestock crop. An extremely fast-growing plant, kudzu now spreads as a noxious weed at the rate of 150,000 acres a year, effectively shading and killing native plants in its way. Under ideal conditions, kudzu can grow 60 feet each year at a rapid pace of about 1 foot per day. Southerners say that you have to close your windows at night to keep the kudzu out. Covering millions of acres in the South, kudzu has now reached northward into southern Ontario. Industrious Southerners use kudzu to make baskets, soaps, and foods.

LEATHERFLOWER
Clematis viorna
Buttercup family (Ranunculaceae)
Quick ID: reddish-purple urn-shaped flowers, heart-shaped leaves, sprawling vine to 12'

Upon careful inspection you may notice that the elegant urn-shaped flowers of leatherflower are actually formed by the upturned sepals rather than true petals. Butterflies visit the hidden flower parts found under the sepals. The 4 reddish-purple sepals are tough and leathery, hence the name leatherflower. The genus name *Clematis* is from an ancient Greek word that means "climbing plant." The vines of *Clematis* climb gracefully over fences and small bushes, produce their flowers in summer, and are enjoyed by chipmunks that devour the succulent flower heads. In late summer and fall, the seeds appear as inflated clusters of whitish feathery puffs resembling an old man's beard and are quite noticeable along the road.

VIRGIN'S BOWER
Clematis virginiana
Buttercup family (Ranunculaceae)
Quick ID: 3 sharply toothed leaflets, 4-petaled white flowers

In August the hot summer breeze is filled with the sweet fragrance of virgin's bower. Trailing over fencerows and other shrubs, the 12- to 15-foot vines climb gently over their supports while producing lavish clusters of starry white flowers. In fall grayish plumes of feathery seeds that resemble large powder puffs covering the roadsides follow the white flowers, leading some to call this plant "old man's beard" or the "devil's darning needles." Although all parts of the plant are poisonous, Native Americans used an infusion of virgin's bower and milkweed for backaches. They also used it as an ingredient for a ceremonial medicine during the Green Corn Ceremony, when the annual corn harvest was celebrated.

VIRGINIA CREEPER
Parthenocissus quinquefolia
Grape family (Vitaceae)
Quick ID: 5 palmate toothed leaflets 4"–8" across; bluish-black berries; small, greenish flowers

Often mistaken for poison ivy, Virginia creeper has 5 leaves rather than the characteristic 3 leaves of poison ivy. In the same family as grapes, the leaves of Virginia creeper do not contain urushiol, the oil that causes skin irritation due to contact with poison ivy. In fall the leaves of Virginia creeper turn deep red and act as a banner on which to display the stemmed dark-blue berries. The berries are toxic to humans, but birds and other wildlife eat them without ill effect, and they are an important source of winter food. The vine can easily climb up rock cliffs as well as trees and shrubs due to specialized tendrils equipped with small adhesive pads.

WILD GRAPE
Vitis sp.
Grape family (Vitaceae)
Quick ID: leaves vary by species from heart-shaped to round and serrated to lobed or unlobed, form looping woody vines climbing to 70' via tendrils

Wild grapes have long provided both humans and wildlife a readily available source of fresh fruit. Grapes are widely used to make jellies, jams, and juice. Wild grapes are also used to make wine. At least 5 species of wild grapes can be found along the Parkway, including fox grape (*V. labrusca*), summer grape (*V. aestivalis*), frost grape (*V. vulpina*), and possum grape (*V. cinerea*), all of which vary in taste and form. Folk remedies called for applying grapevine sap to rid the skin of freckles and also for growing hair. In fall grapevines are collected to be woven as baskets, decorations, and even furniture.

COW PARSNIP
Heracleum maximum
Carrot family (Apiaceae)
Quick ID: large 4"–8" flat clusters of small white flowers; maplelike leaves up to 12"; very tall, grooved, hairy stem
Height: 3'–10'   Bloom season: June–August

With gigantic proportions, cow parsnip towers above all other flowers along the Parkway. The genus name, *Heracleum,* means "Hercules," and the species name, *maximum,* refers to the plant's great size. Growing up to 10 feet tall, the flat-topped white flower is found throughout most of the United States except the Gulf Coast and southernmost eastern states. The hairy foliage and stems can cause a sunburn-like rash. Native Americans ate the peeled stalks like celery, either raw or cooked. The roots were pounded and used to make poultices to apply to sores or bruises. The roots were also used to make a yellow dye. Cow parsnip is eaten by white-tailed deer, and although favored by cows, it is toxic to them.

BUTTERFLY WEED
Asclepias tuberosa
Dogbane family (Apocynaceae)
Quick ID: alternate pointed leaves, bright-orange clustered flowers
Height: 1'–2' Bloom season: June–August

Butterfly weed or butterfly milkweed grows in sunny meadows and fields throughout the Parkway. The striking bright-orange flower clusters attract hummingbirds and butterflies. Native Americans used the root as a treatment for pleurisy and other lung ailments; in fact this plant is sometimes called pleurisy root. Poisonous in large doses, it contains a cardiac glycoside, which is a chemical that affects the heart and other body systems. This plant is becoming scarce in many areas due to illegal digging. Please leave it for others to enjoy.

COMMON MILKWEED
Asclepias syriaca
Dogbane family (Apocynaceae)
Quick ID: pinkish flowers in round clusters; opposite oval leaves, hairy underneath
Height: 3'–5' Bloom season: June–August

Common milkweed grows throughout the summer months in open fields and meadows. As a defense mechanism, common milkweed contains toxic milky-white sap to deter insects and other predators from eating the plant. Monarch butterflies are immune to the toxins and lay their eggs on the plant. When the caterpillars eat the plant leaves, they accumulate the toxins in their body. After the adult butterfly emerges, it still contains the toxins, and birds soon learn that monarchs have a terrible taste. In autumn teardrop-shaped brown pods develop that eventually break open and release the seeds, which are attached to long, white, feathery hairs that carry the seeds away on the autumn breeze.

JACK-IN-THE-PULPIT
Arisaema triphyllum
Arum family (Araceae)
Quick ID: 3 oval leaflets atop the stem, spike of tiny flowers covered by light-green hood with white or purplish stripes
Height: 8"–24"   Bloom season: April–June

The unusual appearance of the Jack-in-the-pulpit makes it one of the easiest spring wildflowers to identify. The tiny flowers are found on a fleshy spike called a spadix. The spadix is surrounded by a showy bract called a spathe. The spathe acts as a protective umbrella for the tiny, inconspicuous flowers held on the fingerlike spadix. Jack-in-the-pulpits are quite variable. Some have whitish stripes on the spathe while others have purplish stripes. Some of the plants growing in boggy areas are deeply ridged or fluted, while others that grow in rich woods lack obvious ridges. The underground corms contain calcium oxalate crystals that cause immediate pain when chewed, but Native Americans did dry them for use as food.

BLACK-EYED SUSAN
Rudbeckia hirta
Aster family (Asteraceae)
Quick ID: bright-yellow ray flowers, dark-blackish-brown center, alternate lance to oval bristly hairy leaves, bristly hairy stem
Height: 1'–3' Bloom season: June–October

A lovely but often overlooked wildflower is the black-eyed Susan that quietly brightens meadows and open areas along the Parkway. This and other yellow daisy-like flowers are composed of 2 types of flowers. The outermost bright yellow "petals" are called ray flowers and are designed to attract a wide variety of pollinators. The disk flowers make up the black or dark-brown center, often with a ring of tiny yellow blossoms showing the yellow pollen. The bristly hairs on the stem and leaves act as a deterrent for insects such as nectar-robbing ants. Native Americans used the roots of black-eyed Susan for earaches and to bathe sores and snakebites.

BRISTLY ASTER
Symphyotrichum puniceum
Aster family (Asteraceae)
Quick ID: bluish-purple to whitish flowers with yellow or reddish center, oblong leaves hairy below
Height: 2'–7' Bloom season: August–October

Found in wet meadows and moist places, bristly aster accompanies the changing colors of fall foliage. Asters belong to a huge family with more than 20,000 species in the world, of which there are about 4,800 species in North America. About 14 species of asters have been found along the Blue Ridge Parkway. Based on DNA sequencing, many common asters in North America are now placed in the genus *Symphyotrichum* rather than the genus *Aster,* including bristly aster. In some older wildflower field guides, this species may be listed as purple-stemmed aster, *Aster patens.* According to mythology asters were formed from the fallen tears of the Greek goddess Virgo.

SKUNK GOLDENROD
Solidago glomerata
Aster family (Asteraceae)
Quick ID: relatively large, rounded yellow flower heads
Height: 1'–5' Bloom season: July–October

About 35 species of goldenrod can be found along the Parkway, but telling them apart is a challenge even for botanists. Found only in the high mountains of the Appalachians, skunk goldenrod is also known as clustered goldenrod in reference to the clusters of relatively large 1 to 10 flowers per stem. The common name, skunk goldenrod, is not undeserved as the fragrance reminds you of the musky smell of a skunk. Restricted in range to eastern Tennessee and western North Carolina, skunk goldenrod grows in open spruce woods at high elevations such as Mount Mitchell State Park. Many other species of goldenrod can be found along the Parkway, including tall goldenrod (*S. altissima*) and common goldenrod (*S. nemoralis*).

WHITE SNAKEROOT
Ageratina altissima
Aster family (Asteraceae)
Quick ID: oval leaves with long points, white flat-topped flowers
Height: 1'–5' Bloom season: July–October

Found in rich woods throughout the Parkway, white snakeroot is a commonly seen but often overlooked flower. The common name, snakeroot, is derived from its use as a remedy for snakebites. White snakeroot is considered a weed in farmlands and pastures. The foliage and roots are toxic and can cause a potentially fatal illness called milk sickness if humans drink the milk of cattle that have eaten the plant. This plant has recently undergone a name change from *Eupatorium rugosum*, as the genus has recently undergone taxonomic revision by botanists.

SPOTTED JEWELWEED
Impatiens capensis
Touch-me-not family (Balsaminaceae)
Quick ID: oval coarsely toothed leaves, orange flowers with spur
Height: 2'–5'   Bloom season: July–September

Spotted jewelweed flowers brighten moist areas along the Parkway, adorning creek sides with graceful orange flowers. Often used by settlers and Native Americans, the juice of this plant helps relieve the itch of poison ivy and mosquito bites and reduces the sting of stinging nettle. Also called spotted touch-me-not, the slightest touch will make the mature seedpods pop with explosive action, flinging the seeds up to 5 feet away. The related pale touch-me-not, *I. pallida*, has yellow flowers.

FIRE PINK
Silene virginica
Pink family (Caryophyllaceae)
Quick ID: 5 narrow, notched, scarlet-red petals; downy sticky stems; basal leaves form rosette, stem leaves opposite unstalked lance-shaped
Height: 12"–30" Bloom season: April–June

The color red is said to influence emotions of both love and hate, and a wildflower called fire pink may elicit both of these in the natural world. Hummingbirds have learned that red tubular flowers often offer nectar, and the scarlet-red flowers of fire pink advertise their savory sweetness in a covert exchange for pollination. The stems of this flower are covered in short sticky hairs that trap and deter crawling insects from reaching the nectar source. This helps to ensure that only hummers and other special-ized flying insects receive the nectar instead of crawling insects that are ineffective pollinators for this plant. "Catchfly" is a common name that refers to the sticky insect-trapping hairs on the stems.

GALAX

Galax urceolata
Diapensia family (Diapensiaceae)
Quick ID: spike of small white flowers; long thin stalk; dark-green, heart-shaped, shiny
leaves 2"–5"
Height: 1'–2.5'   Bloom season: May–July

Galax is a gracefully beautiful plant found in the Appalachian Mountains. The genus name *Galax* comes from the Greek word *gala,* which means "milk," referring to the milky-white color of the flowers. Famous for country music, the town of Galax, Virginia, was named for this plant. Because the leathery leaves are used in holiday floral arrangements, galax is one of the plants that is often poached along the Blue Ridge Parkway. It is illegal to pick, dig, or disturb any plant along the Parkway, and illegal harvest of these and other plants is threatening their populations. Please leave these and other flowers for others to enjoy. Please alert a park official if you see illegal harvesting of any plants.

INDIAN PIPE
Monotropa uniflora
Heath family (Ericaceae)
Quick ID: translucent, waxy white flower and stem, nodding urn-shaped flowers, blackens with age
Height: 2"–10"   Bloom season: June–September

A strange-looking but amazing little flower, Indian pipe, or ghost plant, has found a way to survive even though it lacks a mechanism to undergo photosynthesis. Without the ability to produce its own food, Indian pipe leaches sugars from a fungus. The fungus, either a *Russula* or a *Lactarius*, forms a mutually favorable relationship with tree roots that supply the fungus with sugars, and in return the fungus helps the tree absorb water and minerals. This complex triangled relationship results in the ability of the Indian pipe to survive in the dense understory of rich woods where little sunlight reaches the forest floor. The plant turns black with age and dissolves into gelatinous goo.

SCARLET BEE BALM
Monarda didyma
Mint family (Lamiaceae)
Quick ID: clusters of whorled scarlet tubular flowers, square stem, opposite serrated oval leaves
Height: 30"–60" Bloom season: July–August

Complementing the lush green background of summer, the crimson-red flowers of scarlet bee balm are showstoppers for Parkway visitors. Fond of damp areas, these members of the mint family grow in seepage areas and along streambeds, where hummingbirds eagerly seek them out. This plant was also a favorite for Native Americans, who used it medicinally for a wide variety of purposes including stomach ailments and as a sedative. A poultice of the leaves was used for headaches and colds as well as relieving the sting from bees. The leaves make a wonderful aromatic tea and were used to flavor Earl Grey tea. The Oswego Indians of New York also drank the tea, leading to the common name "Oswego tea."

FALSE HELLEBORE
Veratrum viride
Lily family (Liliaceae)
Quick ID: large leaves that clasp the tall stem, star-shaped greenish-yellow flowers
Height: 2'–8'   Bloom season: May–July

A tall plant, false hellebore often reaches 6 to 8 feet tall and is a conspicuous plant of wetland and swampy areas. The plant has been used historically for a variety of ailments including high blood pressure, fever, pain, coughs, and constipation. Containing more than 200 different alkaloids, all parts of the plant are highly toxic and cause severe vomiting, low blood pressure, and even death. These chemicals are used by the plant to protect it from potential herbivores. The toxins in false hellebore have been used to kill rats, mice, and lice.

TURK'S CAP LILY
Lilium superbum
Lily family (Liliaceae)
Quick ID: several large orange drooping flowers, spotted reddish-brown petals recurved, tall stem, lance-shaped leaves in whorls
Height: 3'–7' Bloom season: July–August

The tallest member of the lily family, turk's cap lily can reach up to 7 feet tall and can be found adorned by swallowtails in sunny meadows and along roadways and trails. Several reddish-orange lilies can be found along the Parkway, but the extremely recurved petals of turk's cap lily help to identify this eastern native. The common name turk's cap comes from the flower's similarity to a colorful traditional Turkish felt hat with recurved brim and pointed top. The petals of Canada lilies (*L. canadense*) are not as recurved as those of turk's cap lily. The rare Gray's lily (*L. grayi*) has redder petals, and Micheux's lily, or Carolina lily (*L. michauxii*), is typically lighter orange with broader leaves.

169

PINK LADY'S SLIPPER
Cypripedium acaule
Orchid family (Orchidaceae)
Quick ID: single pink pouch-shaped flower with slit in front, leafless stalk, 2 opposite oval basal leaves with grooves
Height: 6"–15"   Bloom season: April–June

What a lovely sight it is in May to see pink lady's slippers gracing the trails and partially shaded banks along the Parkway. It thrives in dry acidic soils, especially in coniferous habitats. The unusual pouch shape of the blossoms reminds you a bit of moccasins, which gave rise to another common name, moccasin flower. Pink lady's slippers are in the orchid family along with yellow lady's slippers (*C. parviflorum*) and the much smaller pink and white showy orchis (*Galearis spectabilis*). If the flower is not allowed to complete its life cycle, it will not regenerate. Please do not pick these or any other flowers along the Parkway.

BLOODROOT
Sanguinaria canadensis
Poppy family (Papaveraceae)
Quick ID: single flower, 8–12 white petals, yellow stamens; leaves deeply lobed
Height: 2"–6" Bloom season: March–April

You may wonder why such a lovely spring wildflower has been given such an intriguing common name as bloodroot. The delicate white petals of bloodroot do not give any hint that within the stem and roots this beauty bleeds a juice the color of blood. A native of rich eastern and Midwestern woodlands, the juice or sap of bloodroot was used by Native Americans as body paint and to make a yellowish-orange dye for clothing and baskets. It was also used for medicinal purposes to treat ulcers, skin sores, and skin cancers. The sap contains a strong alkaloid called sanguinarine that destroys cells. Once used as an antibacterial in toothpaste, current research suggests that the plant actually causes precancerous lesions.

BLACK COHOSH

Actaea racemosa
Buttercup family (Ranunculaceae)
Quick ID: white flower spikes about 12" long, tall pliable stems, leaves coarsely toothed, 3 leaflets
Height: 3'–8' Bloom season: June–September

Summer roadsides are filled with the tall spikes of black cohosh that bend and sway in the breeze of passing vehicles. Long used as an aid for female problems and other maladies, Native Americans passed on the medicinal use of black cohosh to early colonists. It was used for fevers, bronchitis, and rheumatism and was an ingredient of the "snake oil" touted by traveling salesmen as a cure-all. It is currently used as an herbal supplement for menopausal symptoms, but the safety and efficacy of this plant have not been confirmed. The tiny blue Appalachian azure butterfly lays its eggs on the flower buds of black cohosh, which provides a ready-made meal for the caterpillars when they hatch.

WILD COLUMBINE

Aquilegia canadensis
Buttercup family (Ranunculaceae)
Quick ID: nodding red-and-yellow flowers with 5 upward spurs; long, slender stems; 3-lobed leaflets
Height: 1'–3' Bloom season: April–September

Partners with the breeze, the distinctive flowers of wild columbine duck and bob about on slim, flexible stems. The showy nodding flower has 5 red backward-pointing spur-like petals with yellow borders. The red-and-yellow flowers are visited by flitting ruby-throated hummingbirds as they briefly join in the air dance, sipping sweet nectar from the tubular red spurs. Before darting off, the hummingbird unknowingly gathers pollen on its head to be delivered to the next columbine to support pollination. Columbines can be seen all along the Parkway on rocky banks and hillsides. This is the only columbine native to eastern North America, but it has several cousins in the western states with colors that range from yellow to blue.

GOAT'S BEARD
Aruncus dioicus
Rose family (Rosaceae)
Quick ID: arching plumes of tiny creamy-white 5-petaled flowers; alternate compound leaves with double-toothed edges
Height: 3'–6' Bloom season: May–July

Goat's beard is a conspicuous plant often seen waving in the breeze of passing motorists along the Parkway. The tall stems gracefully hold the spray of creamy-white flowers that resemble Fourth of July sparklers. Also called bride's feathers, the male and female flowers are borne on separate plants. Producing numerous stamens per flower, the males produce a showier bloom than the less extravagant female plants, with only 3 parts per flower. Often growing in dense colonies, goat's beard can be seen under dappled shade in rich, moist wooded areas. The genus name *Aruncus* comes from the Greek word for "goat's beard" and refers to the feathery clusters of flowers. The specific epithet (species) name *dioicus* refers to separate male and female flowers.

APPALACHIAN BLUETS
Houstonia serpyllifolia
Bedstraw family (Rubiaceae)
Quick ID: mats of tiny sky-blue 4-petaled flowers with yellow center, round to oval leaves
Height: 2"–8" Bloom season: April–July

Throughout the Parkway shaded pathways are brightened by tiny color-ful sky-blue flowers called bluets. Also known as thyme-leaved mountain bluet or creeping bluet, the intense blue flowers of Appalachian bluets attract the attention of hikers along dense forest trails. They spread by runners called rhizomes and often form large colonies that blanket moist forested areas. Quaker ladies (*H. caerulea*) have leaves that look like tiny spatulas, and their coloration is lighter blue to bluish white. The genus *Houstonia* was named to honor Dr. William Houston, an English bota-nist who researched and collected tropical plants. Look for bluets along trails and walkways in spring and early summer.

COMMON MULLEIN
Verbascum thapsus
Snapdragon family (Scrophulariaceae)
Quick ID: rosette of large wooly leaves, yellow flowers on a tall spike
Height: 2'–8' Bloom season: June–September

Native to Europe, northern Africa, and Asia, common mullein was introduced to the United States by early colonists and is now a familiar tall
flower of waste places and fields throughout most of the country. In summer the yellow flowers that adorn the tall stalks attract insects and butterflies. During the Revolutionary War the seeds, which contain rotenone,
were used by settlers to paralyze fish for easy collection. The large wooly
leaves had many uses including warm padding for shoes, a poultice for
rheumatism, and even as toilet paper. A tea was made from the plant to be
used as a remedy for whooping cough and asthma. The tall stalks were
dipped in tallow and used as torches.

PAINTED TRILLIUM
Trillium undulatum
Trillium family (Trilliaceae)
Quick ID: 3 white petals with reddish V-shaped markings in center
Height: 8"–16" Bloom season: April–May

For wildflower lovers visiting the Parkway in early spring, the appearance of graceful trillium blooms is one of the exceptional highlights. Beginning in April, these extraordinary wildflowers unfurl their blossoms and leaves in multiples of 3. The 7 species of trillium that can be found along the Parkway are either white or red, with some turning pink with age. Painted trillium has white petals emblazoned with unique reddish V-shaped blazes at the base of each petal. Found in rich woodlands, look for trilliums near Mabry Mill (MP 176.1), Moses Cone Memorial Park (MP 294.1), Julian Price Memorial Park (MP 297.1), and Crabtree Falls (MP 339.5). Please remember it is illegal to pick or damage any wildflower in the park.

Grasses are a vitally important source of food for many animals as well as humans. Grasses have jointed stems while the stems of sedges and rushes lack joints. The stems of sedges have edges and those of rushes are round. Sedges and rushes are usually found in areas with high moisture content, such as along streambeds and wetlands.

Quick ID for Grasses, Sedges, and Rushes

	Family	Stem
Grasses	Poaceae	Jointed, usually round
Sedges	Cyperaceae	Lacking joints, usually triangular
Rushes	Juncaceae	Lacking joints, rounded and solid

FRASER'S SEDGE
Carex fraseriana
Sedge family
(Cyperaceae)
Quick ID: long, glossy, evergreen strap-like leaves; long stems; white pom-pom-like flowers
Height: 12"–16"

Sedges are very common and important members of the forest community but are often misidentified as grasses. Typically the stems of sedges have triangular wedges and straight, narrow leaves. Often associated with rhododendrons, a southern Appalachian endemic called Fraser's sedge is an unusual sedge with white cottony blooms and strap-like leaves.

BOTTLEBRUSH GRASS
Elymus hystrix
Grass family (Poaceae)
Quick ID: alternate bristle-tipped seeds look like a bottlebrush
Height: 2.5'–3'

Native to eastern and central North America, the bottlebrush grass is one of the easiest to identify as the bristly-tipped seeds give the appearance of a bottlebrush on a long stem. Grasses provide food and cover for many animals including birds, rabbits, and deer.

BRACKEN FERN
Pteridium aquilinum
Bracken fern family (Dennstaedtiaceae)
Quick ID: large; long, arching stem; leaves at end divided into 3 triangular parts
Height: 2'–6'

If any plant could be considered a world traveler, it would be bracken fern, which has been found on every continent except Antarctica. This cosmopolitan fern has a long, successful history as its ancestors left their mark in the fossil record more than 55 million years ago. Bracken has a long list of human and animal uses including thatch roofing, fuel, and livestock bedding. It has also been used as a food and for brewing beer. The rhizomes were used to make a yellow dye and were dried and used as a substitute for flour and for treatment for parasitic worms. It is now known that bracken fern causes stomach and esophageal cancer and should be avoided.

HAYSCENTED FERN
Dennstaedtia punctilobula
Bracken fern family
(Dennstaedtiaceae)
Quick ID: deciduous fronds, single
unclustered, yellowish-green, lacy,
narrow-triangular
Height: 1'–2'

If you brush your fingers
along lacy fronds of this fern,
the familiar aroma of freshly
cut hay fills the air. Hayscented fern is common along trails, sometimes
forming large pale-green colonies that fill open woods and clearings. The
family name, Dennstaedtiaceae, honors German botanist August Wil-
helm Dennstaedt (1776–1826).

CHRISTMAS FERN
Polystichum acrostichoides
Wood fern family
(Dryopteridaceae)
Quick ID: evergreen, fronds lance-shaped,
tapering leaflets eared at base
Height: 1'–3'

Christmas fern is one of the most
common ferns along the Parkway
and one of the easiest to identify.
The shiny, leathery fronds grow
in bouquet-like circular clusters
from a central rootstock. The leaflets are eared at the base and form
tiny boots that resemble Christmas stockings.

MOUNTAIN WOODFERN
Dryopteris campyloptera
Wood fern family
(Dryopteridaceae)
Quick ID: large light-green, lacy
triangular fronds; deciduous
Height: 2'–3'

A unique fern that has genes
from 2 different species, the
mountain woodfern is only
found at high elevations along the Parkway such as the Black Balsam area.
One parent, intermediate woodfern (*D. intermedia*), is common along the
Parkway, but the other parent, spreading woodfern (*D. expansa*), is found
much further north and is no longer found in the southern Appalachians.

FIELD HORSETAIL
Equisetum arvense
Horsetail family (Equisetaceae)
Quick ID: variable, some stems with
whorled branches, some producing a ter-
minal spore-bearing cone-like structure
(strobilus)
Height: 6"–18"

Horsetails may be one of the most
ancient plants, towering to tree
size during the Carboniferous
period, and their decomposed
remains provide the world's coal,
oil, and gas. The common name
"horsetail" and the Latin name
Equisetum come from the resem-
blance of the plant to a horse's tail. Native Americans made use of the
stems, which contain silica, to polish and scour various objects.

APPALACHIAN FIRMOSS
Huperzia appalachiana
Clubmoss family
(Lycopodiaceae)
Quick ID: evergreen clustered upright finger-shaped spikes, narrow triangular leaves
Height: 2.4"–4"

Known as fern allies, firmosses and clubmosses have more primitive characteristics than true ferns. Also known as mountain firmoss, Appalachian firmoss is restricted to high-elevation rock outcrops. These exposed cliffs and rock outcrop habitats have become a source of concern for Parkway biologists. These and other unique plants are sometimes trampled by visitors enjoying the views without realizing the harm they may be causing to the fragile life forms that exist in these extreme conditions.

FAN CLUBMOSS
Diphasiastrum digitatum
Clubmoss family
(Lycopodiaceae)
Quick ID: leaves form flattened branching fans, ground-hugging stem up to 4'
Height: 6"–19"

Millions of years ago ancient clubmoss relatives reached 100 feet in height, but now we use their fossilized remains as a source of power known as coal. Fan clubmoss is also called groundcedar or Southern running-pine as it resembles miniature cedar boughs. The spores that are borne on tall branches called strobili are flammable and were once used as flash powder for photography.

CINNAMON FERN
Osmunda cinnamomea
Royal fern family
(Osmundaceae)
Quick ID: arching circular clusters of fronds, frond broadest near middle tapering to point at tip, separate erect fertile spike of brownish spores
Height: 1'–4'

Most ferns have their spores on the underside of their leaflets, but cinnamon fern is an exception to the rule with long club-like fertile spikes producing the spores. From a distance, the fertile spikes resemble cinnamon sticks, hence the common name. Interrupted fern (*O. claytonii*) is similar, but the spore masses are produced about ⅓ up the frond leaf.

APPALACHIAN ROCK POLYPODY
Polypodium appalachianum
Polypody family
(Polypodiaceae)
Quick ID: evergreen lance-shaped fronds widest near base, waxy leaflets begin about ⅓ up the stem, leaf tips relatively pointed
Height: 6"–12"

Rocky slopes and cliffs are the favored habitat for many of the polypody ferns, which number about 100 species worldwide with 11 species in North America. Thanks to genetic research, the Appalachian rock polypody is a newly recognized species long thought to be the same as rock polypody (*P. virginianum*).

WIND SWEPT MOSS
Dicranum sp.
Broom moss family
(Dicranaceae)
Quick ID: shiny green leaves, long and narrow, growing in 1 direction

Luxurious carpets of mosses blanket many rocks and trees as well as filling in ground space between larger forest plants. Mosses lack a vascular system and therefore require high moisture, but many mosses can survive months of dryness. Mosses produce spores in beak-like capsules on thin stalks.

BOREAL LEAFY LIVERWORT
Bazzania trilobata
Lepidozia family
(Lepidoziaceae)
Quick ID: grows in clumps or mats on moist ground or logs, upper leaves overlap the lower leaves

Leafy liverworts look like mosses and have a similar life cycle, but if you look closely at the leaflets, they are typically in 2 ranks with a smaller third row on the back of the stem rather than the spiral leaflet arrangement of mosses. This gives them the appearance of a millipede and leads to the common name of millipede plant for the boreal leafy liverwort.

RED-FRUITED PIXIE CUP
Cladonia pleurota
Reindeer and cup lichen
family (Cladoniaceae)
Quick ID: tiny pale-yellowish-green
funnel-shaped cups with bright-red
margins, granular hollow stalks
Type: fruticose (shrubby)

Conspicuous in the Lilliputian world of dark-green mosses, the tiny funnels of red-fruited pixie cups appear to have been dipped in bright-red paint. Very similar to the British Soldier lichens (*Cladonia* sp.), the red margins around the cups are the reproductive structures of the fungus.

REINDEER LICHEN
Cladina sp.
Reindeer and cup lichen
family (Cladoniaceae)
Quick ID: whitish to silvery grayish, cushion mounds
Type: fruticose (shrubby)

On open, dry hillsides along the Parkway, you may notice mats of silvery mounds growing a few inches high on thin soil. If you look closely at this lichen, you will see small stems with branches that look like tiny deer antlers, hence the name reindeer lichen. Of course, reindeer are not found on the Blue Ridge Parkway, but in the far north both reindeer and caribou rely on this lichen as an important source of food.

LUNGWORT
Lobaria pulmonaria
Lungwort family
(Lobariaceae)
Quick ID: bright green when moist, brownish when dry, leafy with ridges
Type: foliose (leafy)

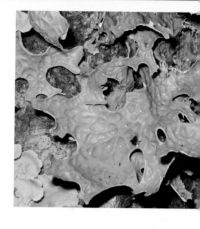

In the early 1600s it was widely believed that the appearance or character of a plant would determine its use. According to this Doctrine of Signatures, lungwort with ridges and pits that resemble lungs could be used to treat respiratory problems. Sensitive to air pollution, lungworts are composed of a unique symbiosis between a fungus, a green algae, and a cyanobacterium.

BUSHY BEARD LICHEN
Usnea strigosa
Parmelia family
(Parmeliaceae)
Quick ID: long pale-yellowish-green bristly strands, tips with yellowish hairy cups
Type: fruticose (shrubby)

Lichens possess a wide array of chemicals to fend off predators such as bacteria that would destroy them. These antibacterial properties are being studied as sources of medicines and other valuable uses. Usnic acid is one such chemical in beard lichens that shows promise in the treatment of wounds and burns.

COMMON GREENSHIELD LICHEN
Flavoparmelia caperata
Parmelia family (Parmeliaceae)
Quick ID: pale-yellow-green lobes with irregular granular patches, lower surface black
Type: foliose (leafy)

A familiar lichen that typically grows on trees, the common greenshield lichen can be found throughout the Parkway. The very similar rock greenshield lichen (*F. baltimorensis*) grows on rocks.

CAROLINA NAVEL LICHEN
Umbilicaria caroliniana
Umbilicate family (Umbilicariaceae)
Quick ID: grows on rocks, looks like tiny greenish-brown folded ears, rubbery when wet,
lower surface black with granules
Type: foliose (leafy)

Carolina navel lichen grows on exposed rocks at high elevations along the
Blue Ridge. The only other place it grows is in northern Yukon and the
adjacent Brooks Range in Alaska. Once widespread, most populations of
this lichen were wiped out during the last ice age.

COKER'S AMANITA
Amanita cokeri
Amanita family (Amanitaceae)
Quick ID: white cap with pointed white to brownish warts, white stem, white gills, partial veil may cover gills

Many mushrooms first emerge from the ground with a membranous covering called a veil. Many members of the Amanita family retain bits of the veil on the cap and around the stem. Found in oak and pine forests, Coker's amanita is a white Amanita with pointed warts on the cap and distinctive rings around the base of the stalk. Over half of the cases of mushroom poisoning are from this family, including Coker's amanita.

DESTROYING ANGEL
Amanita bisporigera
Amanita family (Amanitaceae)
Quick ID: smooth white cap, white stalk with membranous white ring (annulus), white "sac" around base (volva), white gills

As a symbol of purity, white does not always signify innocence, as the white mushroom called the destroying angel or death angel has earned its name with fatal consequences. A beauty among its peers, this brilliant white mushroom radiates on the forest floor with a lovely lacy stalk skirt called an annulus and a white sac around the base called a volva. However, do not let this innocent demeanor fool you, as one bite will ultimately cause death. Highly poisonous, the toxin called amanitin attacks the liver, central nervous system, and kidneys, killing the unfortunate victim within a week unless a liver transplant can be performed. Do not consume any mushroom unless you are absolutely sure of its identification.

FLY AGARIC
Amanita muscaria
Amanita family (Amanitaceae)
Quick ID: yellow-orange cap with buffy-white dots, creamy-white gills, scurfy-whitish stalk with concentric scaly rings

With a colorful yellowish cap and white warty dots, the fly agaric is one of the most well-known mushrooms in the world. This mushroom has a number of color variations, with the red-capped fly agaric of *Alice in Wonderland* fame more commonly found in the western states. The mushroom is poisonous and hallucinogenic as it contains 2 toxins, ibotenic acid and muscimol, and can be mistaken for the potentially deadly panther cap amanita (*A. pantherina*).

SMOOTH CHANTERELLE
Cantharellus lateritius
Chanterelle family (Cantharellaceae)
Quick ID: orange to yellowish orange, funnel-shaped, blunt ridges under cap onto stalk, grows singly in groups on ground

Chanterelles are delicious edibles that can be found in late summer and early fall, typically in association with oaks. Their orange coloration and funnel shape helps the lucky mushroom hunter find these tasty morsels. The poisonous jack-o-lantern mushroom (*Omphalotus olearius*) is very similar but has sharp forked gills.

BEEFSTEAK FUNGUS
Fistulina hepatica
Tube fungi family (Fistulinaceae)
Quick ID: grows like a bracket fungus on trees, brownish red on top, creamy white underneath

Unlike bracket fungi (polypores) that have many holes in the underside, beefsteak fungus has tiny tubes that hang down, and recent DNA studies have shown that it is more closely related to gilled fungi than bracket fungi. It has the look and consistency of a raw steak and even exudes a dull red juice when cut. Although it tastes slightly acidic, it is a popular edible mushroom and is often cooked in stir-fries or stews.

ARTIST'S CONK
Ganoderma applanatum
Conk family (Ganodermataceae)
Quick ID: semicircle growing on wood, brown to gray on top, white underneath

Although this shelf fungus (polypore) can look like half of a thick extra-large pizza glued to a tree stump, it is hard and inedible. Its claim to fame is its use as a canvas for artists' etchings. When the white underside is scratched with a sharp object, it reveals the hard brown pores underneath, which retain their design for years. Please remember that it is illegal to damage or deface any objects in the Parkway, including this fungus.

LING CHIH
Ganoderma lucidum
Conk family (Ganodermataceae)
Quick ID: shiny reddish brown with yellow and white margins, woody, hoof-shaped, grows on deciduous trees

The beautiful reddish top of ling chih, or reishi, is shiny and looks as if it has been varnished or shellacked. A hard, woody shelf fungus, it grows on hardwood trees other than conifers. Revered in the Far East as an herbal medicine, it has been used to treat cancer, heart disease, diabetes, and liver disorders. It is currently in studies to determine the efficacy and safety of its use.

GREEN STAIN FUNGUS
Chlorociboria aeruginascens
Earth tongue family (Helotiaceae)
Quick ID: blue-green cup fungus, green stained wood

Creative artists use pigments from many species of fungi as dyes and stains. This tiny cup fungus contains a pigment called xylindein that stains the wood of oaks, poplar, and ash as well as the western aspens. Prized by woodworking artisans, the bluish-green stained wood was known as "green oak" and was used in the fifteenth century to add color to decorative wooden panels.

HONEY MUSHROOM
Armillaria mellea
Marasmius family (Marasmiaceae)
Quick ID: yellowish-brown, honey-colored; gills whitish; growing in clusters on trees; whitish-brown stem with yellowish ring (annulus); black strings under bark

A fungus of fame, the honey mushroom is the producer of foxfire, the eerie blue-green glow of the night in decaying wood. Sometimes called boot-lace fungus, under the bark it forms long black shoelace-like structures called rhizomorphs that glow at night. A parasite on mostly hardwoods, it causes white rot that eventually kills the tree. Honey mushrooms are poisonous raw but edible after cooking.

WHITE MOREL
Morchella deliciosa
Morel family (Morchellaceae)
Quick ID: brownish conical honeycomb or netlike; hollow stem

One of the most sought-after fungal delicacies, morels have been described as a food of the gods. Sometimes called "merkels" in parts of the Appalachians, the locations of these prized edibles are carefully guarded, but they can often be found in association with hickories, tulip trees, and ash, as well as in old apple orchards. The poisonous false morel (*Gyromitra esculenta*) resembles true morels but has a wrinkled cap that is not attached all the way down the stalk, and the stem is often cottony inside rather than hollow.

ELEGANT DOG STINKHORN
Mutinus elegans
Stinkhorn family (Phallaceae)
Quick ID: fetid odor, pinkish-red stalk with gelatinous brown at end

Emerging from an egg-shaped form, the column of textured pinkish-red fungus grows to about 6 inches tall. The top third of this spongy column is covered with vile brownish slime that has the odor of a carcass. Flies by the hundreds are attracted to the fetid odor and land on the brown slime, which contains the sticky fungal spores that are carried by the fly to another spot where they may sprout a new stinkhorn.

SULPHUR SHELF

Laetiporus sulphureus
Polypore family (Polyporaceae)
Quick ID: orange brackets, yellow edges, grows on trees, especially oaks

One of the most commonly seen bracket fungi growing on trees is the sulphur shelf, also known as "chicken of the woods." The yellowish-orange shelves, which can grow to 10 inches across, are a well-known edible that tastes a bit like chicken, although it can cause nausea in certain people. Members of the genus cause brown rot in trees that eventually leads to their demise.

JACK-O'-LANTERN
Omphalotus illudens
Funnel family (Omphalotaceae)
Quick ID: orange, yellow-orange gills, margin down-curved, in clusters at base of hardwood trees, especially oaks

This brightly colored poisonous mushroom can be found in the late fall. The orange pumpkin coloration generated the name jack-o'-lantern mushroom, alluding to Halloween. The gills contain an enzyme called luciferase that acts on luciferin, a pigment that causes them to glow at night like fireflies. Its bioluminescence is a blue-green color and can be seen in low light.

PINK CORAL MUSHROOM
Ramaria subbotrytis
Coral fungi family (Ramariaceae)
Quick ID: resembles pink coral or cauliflower, fist-size on ground in wooded areas

Typically small and inconspicuous, coral mushrooms are often over-looked, but when they are discovered they often receive accolades of wonder from viewers. Resembling undersea coral or a bunch of pink cauliflower, the pink coral mushroom has numerous forked branches that arise from a clumped base.

WOLF'S MILK SLIME
Lycogala epidendrum
Reticulate slime mold family (Reticulariaceae)
Quick ID: small round spheres, variable color from pink to black, grows on wood

Slime molds produce spores and resemble fungi or molds. They were originally placed in the kingdom Fungi, but recent studies have shown that they are not related to true fungi, and they are now placed in the kingdom Amoebozoa along with amoeboid protozoans. Wolf's milk slime mold oozes a red gel if damaged. The "dog vomit" slime mold (*Fuligo septica*) is a brilliant yellow moving blob that often grows in mulch.

INDIGO MILK CAP
Lactarius indigo
Russula family (Russulaceae)
Quick ID: blue all over, often with concentric whitish rings on the cap; cap turns greenish with age

A lovely surprise in blue, the indigo milk cap is colored dark blue to bluish gray and grows along the roads and trails. When damaged or cut, all members of the genus *Lactarius* ooze milky latex, but in this species the latex is bright blue rather than the typical white color. This edible mushroom can color the foods that it is cooked with blue or bluish-green, which can add some lively fun to your dinner table.

RED RUSSULA
Russula sp.
Russula family (Russulaceae)
Quick ID: cap red (variable), white stem, white gills

More than 700 species of russulas have been identified worldwide, and the caps are a wide variety of colors. Many trees rely on russulas in a mutualistic relationship called mycorrhizal association where both organisms benefit. The tree gains water from the fungus as well as essential nutrients. The fungus gets nourishment from the tree in the form of sugars.

POISON PIGSKIN PUFFBALL

Scleroderma citrinum

Earthball family (Sclerodermataceae)

Quick ID: 1"–4" rounded yellowish-brown spheres, stalkless, thick outer wall with flattened pyramidal warts, purplish black inside

Puffballs vary from marble-size to basketball-size. Spores form inside the puffball and when agitated are released like puffs of smoke through a hole in the exterior wall. Some puffballs such as the giant puffball (*Calvatia gigantea*) are edible when white inside. With the consistency of tofu, they are used in recipes such as puffball Parmesan and stir-fries. The poison pigskin puffball or common earthball is poisonous, and as always, correct identification of any wild mushroom is vital.

PAINTED BOLETE
Suillus pictus
Suillus family (Suillaceae)
Quick ID: brick-red cap, yellow pores underneath, scruffy red and yellowish-white stem

Associated with white pines, the painted bolete is a beautiful addition to the early fall forests. Suillus mushrooms are often slimy on top, a feature that has earned them the nickname "slippery Jack." The painted bolete is a type of Suillus but is typically not slimy.

OAK APPLE GALL
Amphibolips confluenta
Gall wasp family (Cynipidae)
Quick ID: green turning to brown, papery golf-ball-size spheres

Many insects cause oak galls, including gall wasps that lay their eggs on oak twigs. The larvae hatch and tunnel into the plant. The plant over-reacts and rapidly grows thick tissue around the invader to keep it from spreading. The larvae get protection from the gall, and the plant is usually not affected. In spring they exit the gall and fly away as adults.

AZALEA GALL
Exobasidium vaccinii
Exobasidia family
(Exobasidiaceae)
Quick ID: light-green mass on azaleas turning velvety white, then brown and hard

Many plants in the heath family, Erica-ceae, are susceptible to gall formation, including the fungus that causes aza-lea gall. This fungus can also infect blueberries, huckleberries, mountain laurel, and rhododendron, and plants that are wet for long periods with little airflow are more commonly infected. As the fungus infects the plant, it forms a protective mass to isolate the pathogen.

GOLDENROD GALL
Eurosta solidaginis
Peacock fly family (Tephritidae)
Quick ID: large marble size, brown on goldenrod stem

Galls are abnormal outgrowths of tissue due to invasion from insects, fungi, bacteria, or mites. The goldenrod gall fly lays its eggs on a goldenrod, and the larvae tunnel into the stem where the plant forms a benign tumorous gall around a larva. During the long winter months, gall insects are an important source of food for animals such as squirrels and many birds, including chickadees and woodpeckers.

BLACK CHERRY GALL
Apiosporina morbosa
Venturia family
(Venturiaceae)
Quick ID: black, thick, irregular swellings on branches and twigs of cherry trees

Black knot is a fungus that infects cherry and plum trees, causing a thick black swelling gall on the twigs and branches. The gall cuts off the nutrient supply to the twig and causes the death of the twig and sometimes the entire tree.

AMETHYST
Quick ID: purplish crystals
Type: mineral

Amethyst is a type of quartz that is violet to purple. Other types of quartz include citrine, which is yellowish, rose quartz, with a pretty rosy-pink coloration, and milky quartz with milky-white hues. The largest amethyst ever found in North America was from North Carolina. Make sure to check out the interesting rocks and minerals at the Museum of North Carolina Minerals near Spruce Pine, North Carolina, at MP 331 on the Blue Ridge Parkway. Remember it is against Parkway regulations to collect rocks or minerals.

EMERALD
Quick ID: bright transparent green
Type: mineral

This brilliant green gemstone is honored as the official state precious stone of North Carolina. In 1969 the state broke the record for the largest single emerald crystal ever found in North America. Emeralds are a variety of the mineral beryl, and they derive their green coloration from chromium or vanadium.

GARNET
Quick ID: dark brownish red
Type: mineral

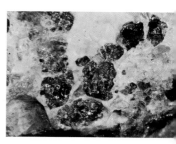

Garnets are a type of silicate mineral formed within other types of rocks, including a type of igneous rock called pegmatite, which is found in nearby mines, including the Spruce Pine mining district. Other semiprecious gemstones such as emeralds and aquamarine can be found in pegmatite.

GNEISS
Quick ID: coarse grained, light- and dark-colored discontinuous layers
Type: metamorphic rock

The banded layer-cake patterns of gneiss (pronounced "nice") reveal a history of transformation immortalized in a textbook of stone. Many millions of years ago, giant continental plates collided, pushing together landforms that were thrust upward and formed the great mountain range we now called the Appalachians. Deep underground the resultant extreme heat and pressure churned and stirred the molten rocks, forming liquid rock composed of various rocks and minerals. Gneiss is one such metamorphic rock that is commonly found along the Parkway.

GRANITE
Quick ID: coarse grained; various shades of gray, white, and black
Type: igneous rock

Igneous rocks such as granite are formed from magma deep below the earth's surface. Granite composes the central core of the Blue Ridge Mountains and provides a strong basement rock that is relatively resistant to the effects of erosion. In 1979 granite was designated as the official state rock of North Carolina due to the rich abundance of this rock in the state. The largest open-face granite quarry in the world is located in Mount Airy, and you can get a great view from MP 202.8 at the overlook View of Granite Quarry. Other views of impressive exposed granite faces include Stone Mountain View at MP 232.5 and Looking Glass Rock at MP 417.1.

GREENSTONE
Quick ID: grayish-green
Type: metamorphic rock

With inconceivable slowness, the continents steadily collided and then drifted apart, forming a base of lava deep under the sea. Under great pressure, basaltic rocks such as greenstone were formed. Catoctin greenstone underlies the first 19 miles of the Parkway. At the Greenstone Overlook at MP 8.8, you can take a short hike along a self-guiding nature trail.

QUARTZITE
Quick ID: variable, gray or white
Type: metamorphic rock

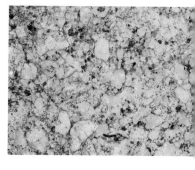

Quartzite is a common metamorphic rock that was formed when sandstone was subjected to the great heat and pressure of colliding tectonic plates. Composed mainly of quartz, quartzite resists erosion and therefore often remains when other rock types erode away by wind and water. Made almost entirely of quartzite, nearby Grandfather Mountain, a biosphere reserve, can be accessed off the Parkway at MP 305 near Linville, North Carolina. At MP 308.3 a quartzite outcrop can be seen at Flat Rock and also at Beacon Heights at MP 305.2.

GLOSSARY

alkaloid: Bitter compounds produced by plants to discourage predators.

alternate leaves: Growing singly on a stem without an opposite leaf.

annulus: Ring or skirt around mushroom stalk formed from remnants of partial veil.

anther: Tip of a flower's stamen that produces pollen grains.

basal: At the base.

bulb: Underground structure made up of layered, fleshy scales.

cache: Storage area of food; to store, as food.

capsule: A dry fruit that releases seeds through splits or holes.

carrion: Remains of deceased animal.

catkin: A spike, either upright or drooping, of tiny flowers.

compound leaf: A leaf that is divided into two or more leaflets.

corm: Rounded, solid underground stem.

crepuscular: Active primarily during dawn and dusk.

crustose: A lichen growth form that is flat.

cryptic: Coloration that allows concealment or camouflage.

deciduous: A plant that seasonally loses its leaves.

detritus: Leaf litter and decaying wood and other organic material mixed with soil.

diurnal: Active by day.

Doctrine of Signatures: A seventeenth-century belief that plants display a sign that indicates their medicinal value.

drupe: Fleshy fruit usually having a single hard pit that encloses a seed.

ecosystem: A biological environment consisting of all the living organisms in a particular area as well as the nonliving components such as water, soil, air, and sunlight.

endemic: Growing only in a specific region or habitat.

ethnobotany: The study of the relationship between plants and people.

evergreen: A tree that keeps its leaves (often needles) year-round.

fledge: When a baby bird leaves the nest after acquiring flight feathers.

foliose: A lichen growth form that appears leafy.

fruticose: A lichen growth form that appears shrubby.

genus: Taxonomic rank below family and above species; always capitalized and italicized.

glean: Pick small insects from foliage.

habitat: The area or environment where an organism lives or occurs.

hawking: Hunting while flying.

hypha (pl., hyphae): Threadlike filaments of fungal cells, basic structural unit of a fungus.

igneous: A type of rock formed from magma or lava that has cooled and solidified.

introduced: A species living outside its native range; often introduced by human activity.

invertebrate: Animals without backbones.

leaflet: A part of a compound leaf; may resemble an entire leaf but it is borne on a vein of a leaf rather than the stem. Leaflets are referred to as pinnae; the compound leaves are pinnate (feather-like).

lichen: A symbiotic association with a fungus and an algae or cyanobacteria.

lobe: A rounded projection.

local resident: Nonmigratory species found year-round in an area; also "resident."

marsupial: Mammals without a placenta that give birth to young who mature in an external pouch.

metamorphic rock: A rock that has been altered by extreme heat and pressure such as gneiss, schist, or quartzite.

mineral: A crystal that is an element or chemical compound formed from geological processes.

mutualism: A type of symbiosis where both organisms benefit.

mycelium: Mass of fungal hyphae that forms the vegetative state of the fungus.

mycorrhiza (pl. mycorrhizae): A symbiotic mutually beneficial relationship between a fungus and the roots of a plant.

nape: Area at the back of the head.

native: A species indigenous or endemic to an area.

nectar: Sweet liquid produced by flowers to attract pollinators.

niche: An organism's response to available resources and competitors (like a human's job).

Glossary

nitrogen fixation: Process by which atmospheric nitrogen is converted by bacteria that reside in plant root nodule into nitrogen compounds that help the plant grow.

nocturnal: Active at night.

omnivore: Feeds on a variety of foods including both plant and animal materials.

opposite leaves: Growing in pairs along the stem.

parasitism: One organism benefits at the expense of another organism.

pinnate: Divided or lobed along each side of a leaf stalk, resembling a feather.

pollen: Small powdery particles that contain the plant's male sex cells.

pollination: Transfer of pollen from an anther (male) to a stigma (female).

primaries: Outermost flight feathers of a bird's wing.

rachis: Main axis or shaft; in plants the main stem of a flower cluster or compound leaf.

rhizome: Underground stem that grows horizontally and sends up shoots.

riparian: Relating to or living in the area between land and a stream or river.

sepal: Usually green leaflike structures found underneath the flower.

simple leaf: A leaf that is not divided into parts.

sinus: Indentations between lobes on a leaf.

species: Taxonomic rank below genus; always italicized but never capitalized; also called "specific epithet."

spine: Modified leaves or stipules that form sharp projections.

stamen: Male part of the flower composed of a filament, or stalk, and anther, the sac at the tip of the filament that produces pollen.

symbiosis: Association of unlike organisms that benefits one or both.

taxonomy: Study of scientific classifications.

thorn: A modified branch or stem that forms a sharp woody projection.

toothed: Jagged or serrated edge.

torpor: Short-term state of decreased physiological activity including reduced body temperature and metabolic rate.

vertebrate: Animal with a backbone.

wing bar: Line of contrastingly colored plumage formed by the tips of the flight feathers of birds.

winged: Thin, flattened expansion on the sides of a plant part.

References

Abramson, R., and J. Haskell, eds. *Encyclopedia of Appalachia.* Knoxville, TN: University of Tennessee Press, 2006.

Alderman, J. A. *Wildflowers of the Blue Ridge Parkway.* Chapel Hill, NC: The University of North Carolina Press, 1997.

Arora, D. *Mushrooms Demystified,* 2nd ed. Berkeley, CA: Ten Speed Press, 1986.

Beane, J. C., A. L. Braswell, J. C. Mitchell, W. M. Palmer, and J. R. Harrison. *Amphibians & Reptiles of the Carolinas and Virginia,* 2nd ed. Chapel Hill, NC: The University of North Carolina Press, 2010.

Bell, R. B., and A. H. Lindsey. *Fall Color and Woodland Harvests.* Chapel Hill, NC: Laurel Hill Press, 1990.

Bolgiano, C. *The Appalachian Forest: A Search for Roots and Renewal.* Mechanicsburg, PA: Stackpole Books, 1998.

Brinkley, E. S. *Field Guide to Birds of North America.* New York: Sterling Publishing Co., 2008.

Brodo, I. M., S. D. Sharnoff, and S. Sharnoff. *Lichens of North America.* New Haven, CT: Yale University Press, 2001.

Brooks, M. *The Appalachians.* Boston: Houghton Mifflin, 1965.

Capinera, J. L., R. D. Scott, and T. J. Walker. *Field Guide to Grasshoppers, Katydids, and Crickets of the United States.* Ithaca, NY: Cornell University Press, 2004.

Catlin, D. T. *A Naturalist's Blue Ridge Parkway.* Knoxville, TN: The University of Tennessee Press, 1984.

Cavender, A. *Folk Medicine in Southern Appalachia.* Chapel Hill, NC: The University of North Carolina Press, 2003.

Clemants, S., and C. Gracie. *Wildflowers in the Field and Forest: A Field Guide to the Northeastern United States.* New York: Oxford University Press, 2006.

Cobb, B. *A Field Guide to Ferns and Their Related Families.* New York: Houghton Mifflin, 1984.

Conant, R., and J. T. Collins. *A Field Guide to Reptiles & Amphibians: Eastern and Central North America,* 3rd ed. New York: Houghton Mifflin, 1998.

Dunkle, S. W. *Dragonflies Through Binoculars: A Field Guide to Dragonflies of North America.* New York: Oxford University Press, 2000.

Eaton, R. E., and K. Kaufman. *Kaufman Field Guide to Insects of North America.* New York: Houghton Mifflin, 2007.

References

Forsyth, A. *Mammals of North America: Temperate and Arctic Regions.* Buffalo, NY: Firefly Books, 2006.

Frick-Ruppert, J. *Mountain Nature: A Seasonal Natural History of the Southern Appalachians.* Chapel Hill, NC: The University of North Carolina Press, 2010.

Glassberg, J. *Butterflies Through Binoculars: The East.* New York: Oxford University Press, 1999.

Harris, A. G., E. Tuttle, and S. D. Tuttle. 2004. *Geology of National Parks,* 6th ed. Dubuque, IA: Kendall/Hunt Publishing Company, 2004.

Howell, P. K. *Medicinal Plants of the Southern Appalachians.* Mountain City, GA: BotanoLogos Books, 2006.

Johnson, Randy. *Best Easy Day Hikes Blue Ridge Parkway,* 2nd ed. Guilford, CT: FalconGuides, 2010.

———. *Hiking the Blue Ridge Parkway,* 2nd ed. Guilford, CT: FalconGuides, 2010.

Kirkman, L. K., C. L. Brown, and D. J. Leopold. *Native Trees of the Southeast.* Portland, OR: Timber Press, 2007.

Little, E. L. *The Audubon Society Field Guide to North American Trees: Eastern Region.* New York: Chanticleer Press, 1980.

Logue, V., F. Logue, and N. Blouin. *Guide to the Blue Ridge Parkway,* 2nd ed. Birmingham, AL: Menasha Ridge Press, 2003.

Lord, W. G. *Blue Ridge Parkway Guide: Grandfather Mountain to Great Smoky Mountains National Park 291.9 to 469 miles.* Birmingham, AL: Menasha Ridge Press, 1981.

———. *Blue Ridge Parkway Guide: Rockfish Gap to Grandfather Mountain 0.0 to 291.9 miles.* Birmingham, AL: Menasha Ridge Press, 1981.

Miller, J. H., and K. V. Miller. *Forest Plants of the Southeast and Their Wildlife Uses.* Rev. ed. Athens, GA: University of Georgia Press, 2005.

Milne, L., and M. Milne. *The Audubon Society Field Guide to North American Insects and Spiders.* New York: Chanticleer Press, 1980.

Page, L. M., and B. M. Burr. *Peterson Field Guide to Freshwater Fishes of North America North of Mexico,* 2nd ed. New York: Houghton Mifflin Harcourt Publishing Company, 2011.

Petrides, G. A. *A Field Guide to Trees and Shrubs,* 2nd ed. New York: Houghton Mifflin, 1986.

Roody, W. C. *Mushrooms of West Virginia and the Central Appalachians.* Lexington, KY: The University Press of Kentucky, 2003.

Sibley, D. A. *National Audubon Society: The Sibley Guide to Birds,* 1st ed. New York: Chanticleer Press, 2000.

Simmons, N. *Best of the Blue Ridge Parkway.* Johnson City, TN: Mountain Trail Press, 2008.

Simpson, M. *Birds of the Blue Ridge Mountains.* Chapel Hill, NC: The University of North Carolina Press, 1992.

Stokes, D. W. *The Natural History of Wild Shrubs and Vines.* New York: Harper & Row, 1981.

Thieret, J. W., W. A. Niering, and N. C. Olmstead. *National Audubon Society Field Guide to North American Wildflowers: Eastern Region.* Rev. ed. New York: Alfred A. Knopf, Inc./Chanticleer Press, 2001.

Virginia Botanical Associates. 2012. *Digital Atlas of the Virginia Flora* (www.va plantatlas.org). c/o Virginia Botanical Associates, Blacksburg, VA.

Webster, W. D., J. F. Parnell, and W. C. Biggs. *Mammals of the Carolinas, Virginia, and Maryland.* Chapel Hill, NC: The University of North Carolina Press, 1985.

Weidensaul, S. *Mountains of the Heart.* Golden, CO: Fulcrum Publishing, 1994.

Wigginton, E., and his students, eds. *Foxfire 3.* New York: Anchor Books/Random House, 1975.

Wilson, D. E., and S. Ruff, eds. *The Smithsonian Book of North American Mammals.* Washington, DC: Smithsonian Institution, 1999.

Index

Index

Index

About the Authors

As professional photographers, biologists, and authors, Ann and Rob Simpson are noted national-park experts, having spent years involved with research and interpretation in US national parks. They have written numerous books on national parks from coast to coast that promote wise and proper use of natural habitats and environmental stewardship. As a former chief of interpretation and national-park board member, Rob has a unique understanding of the  inner workings of the national park system. In cooperation with American Park Network, they have led Canon "Photography in the Parks" workshops in major national parks including Grand Canyon, Yellowstone, Yosemite, and the Great Smoky Mountains.

Ann and Rob are both award-winning biology professors at Lord Fairfax Community College in Middletown, Virginia. With a background in science education, Ann heads the science department, and as part of the college's nature photography curriculum, the Simpsons regularly lead international photo tours to parks and natural history destinations around the world.

Long known for their stunning images of the natural world, their work has been widely published in magazines such as *National Geographic, Time, National Wildlife,* and *Ranger Rick* as well as many calendars, postcards, and books. You can see their work at Simpsons' Nature Photography at www.agpix.com/snphotos.